Tarot Magic

Tarot Magic

A HANDBOOK OF INTUITIVE READINGS, RITUALS, AND SPELLS

FORTUNA NOIR

wellfleet press

First published in 2024 by Wellfleet Press,
an imprint of The Quarto Group,
142 West 36th Street, 4th Floor,
New York, NY 10018, USA
T (212) 779-4972 F (212) 779-6058
www.Quarto.com

Wellfleet titles are also available at discount for retail, wholesale, promotional, and bulk purchase. For details, contact the Special Sales Manager by email at specialsales@quarto.com or by mail at The Quarto Group, Attn: Special Sales Manager, 100 Cummings Center Suite 265D, Beverly, MA 01915 USA.

10 9 8 7 6 5 4 3 2 1

ISBN: 978-1-57715-394-8

Library of Congress Cataloging-in-Publication Data

Names: Noir, Fortuna, author.
Title: Tarot magic : a handbook of intuitive readings, rituals, and spells / [Fortuna
  Noir].
Description: New York, NY, USA : Wellfleet Press, an imprint of The Quarto
  Group, 2024. | Series: Mystical handbook | Includes bibliographical
  references and index. | Summary: "Tarot Magic is the essential
  introduction to this ancient practice, featuring the history of the
  craft alongside practical magic and tarot interpretations that reveal
  the meanings of past, present, and future"-- Provided by publisher.
Identifiers: LCCN 2023023507 (print) | LCCN 2023023508 (ebook) | ISBN
  9781577153948 | ISBN 9780760385555 (ebook)
Subjects: LCSH: Tarot. | Magic.
Classification: LCC BF1879.T2 N584 2024 (print) | LCC BF1879.T2 (ebook) |
  DDC 133.3/2424--dc23/eng/20230623
LC record available at https://lccn.loc.gov/2023023507
LC ebook record available at https://lccn.loc.gov/2023023508

Publisher: Rage Kindelsperger
Creative Director: Laura Drew
Managing Editor: Cara Donaldson
Editor: Elizabeth You
Cover Design: Beth Middleworth
Layout Design: Kim Winscher
Text: Johanie M. Cools

Printed in China

Contents

PROLOGUE

The world of tarot has many faces,
From Kings to Pages to Fives to Aces.

Their varying symbols merge and perplex
Composed of simple and divine objects.

Characters abound, meanings clarified.
Interpretations combine and divide.

Take heart, dear reader, all is well.
Utilize the cards for every spell.

May the Major and Minor guide you,
With this book and the tarot beside you.

Introduction

Tarot cards as we know them today have been around since the 1430s. Originating from Italy, tarot cards began as illustrative playing cards, but over time their use transcended into fortune telling or, as witches call it, a form of divination. A huge misconception about tarot cards is that they show the reader (the practitioner) the exact future of the querent (the inquirer), when in reality this is not the case. As a divination tool, tarot cards rely heavily on established symbolism from the illustrator and the interpretations of the reader or even the querent. Each person sees and responds differently to each card that appears in any reading, whether trivial or significant.

Though there is an established meaning for every card, there's so much more you can get out of it the more you interact with your deck. Once you become more familiar with the cards, their meanings, and their symbols, you will be able to more quickly and accurately read what Spirit is trying to show you. And it doesn't stop there. In today's world there's a plethora of different tarot decks one can use and buy. Some are based on TV shows, books, abstract themes, and myths, or they can be original art. This provides an extra dash of intention for any reading or spells you might perform. But, for the purposes of this book, the spells will be based on the standard Rider-Waite Tarot Deck. It's the deck most beginner witches practice with and will provide the foundation for any additional decks you choose beyond this book. (If you have a deck that's based on the Rider-Waite system, feel free to use that instead.)

Tarot magic doesn't stop at divination; it can and will be used in spellwork as an added layer of intention and meditation. Witchcraft relies heavily on the mind and its capabilities. Tarot cards guide you along, giving you specific images to work with. On their own or combined, they can give you and the Universe the exact message you want to send out. Tarot can aid you in love, luck, money, and more by simply adding them to your spells and using their placements to enhance your practice. Specific placements and order of tarot cards are called spreads. In these pages, you will find the importance of not only picking the right card but also placing it in a certain formation to improve the quality and clarity of each spell or ritual you perform. You can carry cards with you as charms or reminders of your intention.

In every tarot deck, there are seventy-eight cards split into two groups: Major Arcana and Minor Arcana. The Major Arcana has twenty-two cards and the Minor has fifty-six. The difference between the two is their level of importance and specificity. Major Arcana cards generally deal with major themes and areas of life like death, love, tradition, and strength. The Minor Arcana cards deal with everyday challenges and temporary states of being like feeling stressed or relaxed, or facing adversity. Depending on the intensity of your spellwork, you may need only one Major card or several Minor ones. The possibilities are truly endless. With these two groups working in sync, you can combine and tailor them to convey exactly what you want.

Within spellwork, tarot cards can do many things. They can speak the words you may be unable to say, add extra intention to any pre-existing spells you may have in your Book of Shadows, provide you with visual meditation aides, and more. Due to the

nature of the tarot, you can add your own meaning to each card, take away what doesn't speak to you, or focus on a particular aspect of the cards you choose to work with. It's customizable to suit your wants and needs.

Within these pages, we will go over what each individual card means, what their symbols represent, and how to translate them for your personal use. There are many different interpretations of the cards, including what they represent when upright and reversed (upside down). In this book, we will combine many into one to give you a well-rounded and detailed description to better aid you in your card selection.

What you as a reader will gain from this book is a deeper understanding of the tarot, your magic as a whole, and new ways to implement this age-old divination tool. You'll attract love, gain money, open your third eye, and use sabbat magic. Once equipped with this information, you will add a whole new layer to your practice and become a stronger, more knowledgeable, and more confident practitioner. Go and thrive. So mote it be.

Major Arcana

Despite having fewer cards, the Major Arcana portion is the denser half of any tarot deck. They represent major themes, archetypes, and forces affecting us all. When they appear in a reading, take notice because they indicate big changes or running themes in your life. In your practice, they can be used for significant spells with a lot of intention and forethought. Major Arcana cards are much more complex with their meanings and symbols. Depending on what you see, they can tell a simple story or weave a multilayered tale.

Despite the gravity of these cards, feel free to also apply your interpretations to them. This will link the cards to you and add to your overall practice. Before beginning your spellwork, you'll read through the meanings of all twenty-two cards, learn them, and supply your own meanings based on how they speak to you.

To keep track of your interpretations, write them down in your Book of Light or tarot journal. Doing so will help you create your own guide that you can use in your practice indefinitely.

*T*his card is the true first in the deck. The Fool represents new beginnings and unlimited potential. The Fool hasn't gone through too many hardships, as indicated by their clean clothes and fearlessness while on a cliff, so they have a sense of naïveté about them. But with that comes a desire for adventure and optimism. Because of their lack of experience, The Fool can represent someone who's unprepared to deal with upcoming adversities, but that doesn't mean they're not willing to adapt and be flexible. Note that The Fool doesn't have a lot of baggage, which can indicate they're traveling with an open mind and trust the Universe will provide for them, whatever they need. They move when the Sun is high and are willing to take on the world.

When reversed, this card represents negligence, carelessness, and immaturity. Instead of youthful innocence being a good thing, in this position, it translates to being uninformed. Instead of trust, it can represent folly. The Fool may be a person with a sense of adventure and purpose, but they have their head too much in the clouds and don't see reality. They may put themselves in a dangerous position but don't have the self-awareness to realize it. The Fool stands on a ledge as if they were safe on low ground but ignores the ice mountains in the distance despite their ominous presence. Overall, The Fool represents innocence, potential, and fearlessness, whether or not it's warranted.

THE MAGICIAN.

This card is the foundation and master of the Minor Arcana. The Magician has their right hand gripping a wand pointed toward the sky while the left is pointed toward the flora of the earth. This symbolizes the connection between Spirit and our material world. On the table next to The Magician are the suits of the Minor Arcana—a pentacle, a cup, a wand, and a sword—though they're not in order of the deck itself. On their head is the infinity symbol that indicates unlimited potential and combinations of each suit.

When upright, The Magician can represent the querent's creativity, powers of manifestation, and respect for Heaven and Earth. This card also represents responsibility and knowledge of magic as a whole. The Magician uses their wisdom to move about their life, trying to balance their powers. This figure is diplomatic, a teacher, and a magus. Though they have self-confidence, they aren't arrogant. Instead, they have quiet intelligence and use that in an ethical way.

When reversed, The Magician represents a person who is egotistical, someone who believes they know more than everyone else. Instead of trying to be creative for the sake of it, this position represents someone who doesn't want to teach or guide but someone who wants to show off, someone who wants attention and praise. This also lends itself to manipulation and distrust.

The High Priestess depicts a woman who is in tune with the spiritual. She seeks enlightenment from Spirit and to understand the unknown of the Universe. The High Priestess has an element of stillness because she always seeks higher knowledge, as indicated by the Torah on her lap. She sits between two pillars, one with a "B" on it and the other with a "J." The "B" stands for Boaz, which means "He is strong," and the "J" stands for Jachim, which means "God establishes." She also wears a cross over her chest and looks out to the querent with a placid expression.

The High Priestess symbolizes the Feminine Divine as indicated by her garb and the crescent Moon that sits at her feet. Qualities encompassing the Feminine Divine include intuition, spiritual movement, and emotional intelligence. The High Priestess, with her connection to the Moon and her propensity toward the ethereal world, is deeply connected to the supernatural. She is the medium between Spirit and the querent. So, when this card is pulled, it implies mystery, a future that has yet to be revealed, knowledge, and wisdom.

Similar to the Magician, when reversed, this card represents self-importance, arrogance, and surface knowledge. Instead of seeing herself as a vessel for the Universe, she is conceited and seeks to take and take without giving or helping others. Rather than showing others what Spirit wants them to know, she keeps the information close to her chest, leaving the querent unsatisfied and without direction.

3 - THE EMPRESS

This figure represents abundance and peace. The Empress reclines against pillows and blankets comfortably. She is in no rush, feeling completely relaxed and satisfied. Bountiful nature surrounds the Empress in the forms of a rushing waterfall, wheat, and gloriously green trees. Being this relaxed in nature indicates the Empress is in tune with the Earth and her bounty. Atop her head sits a crown with twelve stars, representing the twelve signs of the zodiac, also indicative of the Empress being in harmony with the stars as well as the Earth.

Pulling this card signifies beauty and abundance. Depending on the context of a spell or a reading, this card can either indicate a calm and confident person or tell the querent that they need to relax and allow the world around them to continue as is without trying to control it. The Empress also indicates connecting with

Nature and pursuing what feels natural to you, whether that be artistic pursuits, spending time outdoors, or self-care.

Reversed, the Empress represents light and truth. Not that the upright position means the Empress is dishonest; instead, it denotes pursuing truth and enlightenment instead of relaxation and pleasure. It also represents public rejoicing instead of private contentment as well as indecision and possessive tendencies. Overall, the Empress is a symbol of confidence and positive fortune.

The Emperor represents strength, stability, and authority. Below his royal regalia, he wears armor as though he's ready to fight whenever necessary. The throne the Emperor sits on is made of stone with ram heads adorning it, symbolizing bravery and aggression. In the back are tall mountains, representing a steadfast nature. Nothing can move them. Though these factors may give the impression of a stubborn and unchanging rule, they actually indicate someone who is strong and willing to stand for what they believe to be the fair and right thing to do.

His white beard is a signifier of his age, but that doesn't work against the Emperor. Instead, it is indicative of his wisdom. In his right hand, the Emperor holds an ankh, which is the Egyptian symbol of life. In his left hand is a golden orb representing the world he rules over. Combined, these elements send the message that he is to uphold life and ground the world so it doesn't slip into chaos.

THE EMPEROR.

When upright, this card denotes stability, protection, and conviction—qualities of a good leader. Depending on the context of the spell or reading, it can represent the querent or someone authoritative in the querent's life. It also notes reason and power, which are both necessary to make all important life decisions. When reversed, the Emperor denotes benevolence and compassion, but also selfishness, immaturity, and obstruction. It paints the picture of someone who is kinder, yes, but someone with the capacity to hold others back.

This card is the male version of the High Priestess. Much like the High Priestess, the Hierophant is a spiritual guide, a person likened to a medium. He is a teacher and shepherd of those who look up to him for wisdom and knowledge, as indicated by the two men below. The keys below the Hierophant's feet are the keys to the subconscious and conscious mind. He is well versed in everything supernatural. The crosses on his garb and in his hand signify his religious status and his seat secures his spot as a higher authority.

When upright, this card indicates mercy and goodness. As the Hierophant gets his wisdom from God, he passes on the message that striving for goodness and grace is of the utmost importance. Another signifier is tradition and conformity, which can foster a sense of community. This card may indicate the need to find structure and a unifying force within a person's community.

Reversed, this card represents society at large rather than the confines of a church or temple. Other interpretations are weakness and overkindness. The Hierophant may not have the same appearance as the Emperor, but he is strong nonetheless. However, when reversed, that strength falls away and leaves behind someone who is unsure and more of a pushover rather than an arbiter of truth.

One of the most popular cards in any tarot deck, The Lovers represents the first Biblical couple: Adam and Eve. This card encourages intimacy, as hinted at by the Lovers' nude forms, and a relationship with another person. Above the couple is a grand angel reminding them of God and Heaven while also blessing their union. The Lovers themselves are representative of love that's achieved outside of the norm and is rooted in a deeper understanding of each other, of two people fitting together perfectly.

Upright, this card represents beauty as well as attraction. Love itself is beautiful, but when you're in love, you can more easily see the beauty in someone else. It's a force that brings with it a level of resiliency when a couple allows their love for each other to overcome anything that seeks to separate them.

Reversed, this card denotes temptation, as indicated by the snake behind Eve. Its position leans heavily toward her ear, a sabotaging force accompanying the fruit just above Eve's head. Behind Adam sits a tree on fire, representing the destructive nature of love. When felt too strongly or one-sidedly, it can bring about much harm. This card illustrates that love itself is a double-edged sword.

The Chariot depicts a knight atop a chariot with a staff in their right hand being led by two sphynxes—one black and one white. The rider wears a serious expression with an air of determination. Atop the chariot lies a covering dotted with stars, indicating that the rider is being guided by the spiritual and their intuition. What makes The Chariot a powerful card is that it indicates forward movement in spite of adversity and external interference. The black and white sphynxes are opposite in both color and direction. They hint at the animalistic tendencies of humanity. In order to charge forward, the rider must rein in their carnal side, remain firmly in control, and constantly be aware of their goal and destiny.

When upright, The Chariot signifies relief and guidance. The rider has been on many journeys, as shown by their crown, armor, and the chariot itself. Alternatively, The Chariot denotes triumph over nature and vengeance, a reminder that personal achievement can also include nefarious desires. With this kind of single-mindedness The Chariot displays, it shows a propensity toward war.

Reversed, The Chariot represents defeat and inattentiveness. Without the rider's watchful eye, the chariot can easily be led into chaos or stagnation. The only thing moving the chariot forward is the desires and abilities of the rider. Without that, The Chariot represents a person without ambition, resiliency, or vision of the future.

S trength, similarly to The Chariot, is about internal strength and control. Instead of making a show of it, the person on the card displays quiet and thoughtful strength. The figure holding the lion isn't screaming, crying, or in any way irate. Rather, they hold the lion with a serene expression and a firm but not forceful grip. This type of strength is much more subtle than that of The Chariot. It focuses more on the individual and the strength that comes from Spirit and not just from personal experience.

STRENGTH.

The figure has the courage to grab the lion to prevent it from attacking them and instead holds still, redirecting the lion's will. This is an example of the proper use of power and persuasion to get what one wants. It isn't selfish or weak, but actually takes a great deal of control and maturity.

When upright, Strength denotes bravery and discernment concerning when to use power for the right reasons. On the other hand, when reversed, Strength hints at weakness and abuse of power. Instead of that quiet courage and emotional intelligence, it indicates someone who doesn't know or respect boundaries. It also signifies someone who is overly eager and misdirects their energy, making a mess of themselves and those around them.

A top a snowy mountain stands the Hermit. The card depicts an old, wise, solitary figure with a lamp in one hand and a staff in the other. They look down from their high position toward those below. The Hermit doesn't think they're better than anyone else but instead acknowledges that they've traveled far enough in life that they can see what others can't. The gray of their robe indicates age and the final stages of life. The lamp denotes knowledge and experience acquired after a long life that guides not only the Hermit but also the querent.

Though the Hermit is on their own, it's not from a lack of community but instead as a necessary way to trust their inner voice and intuition. Community is important, but the Hermit relishes isolation because it offers the opportunity for introspection. Despite how far the Hermit has come, they are always looking for more knowledge and life experience.

When upright, The Hermit represents a person with the combined wisdom of the Heavens and the Earth to achieve enlightenment. Unlike the High Priestess and the Hierophant, the Hermit receives most of their knowledge from personal experience rather than messages from Spirit. They don't let what others think deter them from following their hearts.

THE HERMIT.

When reversed, this card denotes fear and ostracism—in other words, being solitary due to fear of the outside world. It indicates someone who lets rules and stipulations govern them instead of trusting themselves.

The Wheel of Fortune is a literal wheel representing the ebbs and flows of fortune. The Wheel itself has the Hebrew characters "Y H V H," which form the unpronounceable name of God. The characters on the inner wheel are the symbols for mercury, sulfur, water, and salt: the building blocks of life. Around the Wheel is a cast of characters, including the Egyptian god of evil, Typhon; a sphynx with a sword that symbolizes knowledge; and Anubis, the Egyptian god of the dead. In the four corners of the card sit signs of the zodiac—Aquarius, the angel; Scorpio, the eagle; Leo, the lion; and Taurus, the bull—reading to gain knowledge. Their wings indicate sudden flight.

When upright, this card denotes blessings and abundance. Everything on the card works with you to signify a good and peaceful stage. Life is constantly moving in cycles of fortune, neutrality, and misfortune; in this position, the card predicts a fortunate cycle. It encourages the querent to have faith that the Universe will work in their favor.

In reverse, the Wheel of Fortune card represents the downward turns of life. It suggests chaos and misfortune that you must prepare yourself for. Additionally, it also leads to overanalyzing the currents of life. Instead of taking each turn as it comes, this position represents reading too much into and oversimplifying the events of your life in an effort to control or understand them when neither might be possible.

Justice as a card and as a concept is about fairness, truth, and appropriate consequences proportionate to each action. The figure in the seat wears red to signify power. In their right hand, they wield a sword that represents action taken. In their left hand, they hold a scale for balance to ensure the punishment fits the crime. Though it may seem as though Justice is primed to punish, it actually seeks the truth first and foremost before moving to make any decisions. In life, we may not always be cognizant of how our choices will manifest, but Justice is a reminder that what we do has an effect that we will feel the repercussions of.

When used in a reading or spellwork, Justice denotes equity and righteousness. It is the embodiment of the hand of Spirit. Though we may not always understand or agree with it, Justice abounds everywhere. This might indicate that your action or the action of another is about to impact you directly or indirectly. If used in a spell, this card can be a message to Spirit to hurry the impact of Justice on someone else.

When in the reversed position, Justice symbolizes bigotry and bias. It ignores the factor of truth and instead wields the sword toward anyone the wielder doesn't like or approve of. It also can be indicative of excessive severity in whatever judgment does come out. Take care to use this card wisely and sparingly, as its effects can be heavy.

This card displays a man hanging upside down from a cross-like tree. At first, it seems as though the Hanged Man has been put in this position unwillingly and is dealing with the consequences of whatever brought him there. This is an incorrect assumption. In actuality, the Hanged Man has placed himself on the cross, as indicated by his relaxed posture and serene expression. The rest of his body is free and there's only one rope holding him in place so that he can easily escape. The halo of light around his head represents enlightenment and a different perspective he wouldn't normally have right side up.

Upright, this card represents introspection and a change in circumstance. There are times when we are so stuck in our heads, we can't find a solution to what troubles us. When this card is pulled, it's a sign telling us to do something unconventional to change how we think about something. By doing so, we may reach a certain realization that gives us the tools to make a positive decision.

Reversed, the Hanged Man's typical action is now passive and used to procrastinate instead of coming up with a solution or seeking knowledge. The once passionate and determined Hanged Man is now content to sit and do nothing. Another interpretation is indifference. In order to reach enlightenment, it's necessary to surrender to Spirit to attain that knowledge. When reversed, this card represents someone who cares nothing for Spirit and chooses inaction.

The Death card is considered by those who don't understand it to be one of the scariest cards in any tarot deck, and understandably so. The card features a living skeleton in black armor marching forward in spite of the priest, parent, and child fearing for their lives. However, Death doesn't only symbolize actual death. Instead, it represents the end of a cycle—birth and rebirth—and transformation, which are all pretty frightening. The black armor the skeleton wears represents the mysteries of death as well as its strength as an impenetrable force. Nothing can harm or stop Death.

Despite the terrifying appearance, Death is a necessary phase so that new life can begin. The flag Death holds is a white flower with five points representing life and the stages of a flower: seed, bud, bloom, wilt, death, and repeat. Many are too afraid of Death to consider all the good it can bring.

When upright, Death symbolizes the end of a major cycle in your life or a call to let go of whatever is holding you back or no longer serves you. Similar to a flower, we need to be pruned in order to bloom more effectively. Something must be left behind. Reversed, Death can mean lethargy or inertia. Instead of actively severing ties, this can indicate you're letting relationships or your own growth die because you aren't putting in the work to keep them alive. In this way, Death does not represent the good but is a sign of something amiss.

DEATH.

Temperance as a card is complicated because the theme and message don't intuitively mesh. Temperance is defined as having restraint, and in tarot, it means having balance and patience. The figure on this card is of a tall, nonbinary angel standing with one foot balanced on a rock and the other inside the lake, symbolizing the balance between logic (earth) and emotion (water). In the angel's hands are two gold chalices with water pouring into one from the other. This represents the constant flow of life from one end to the next. Behind the angel is a path leading up to a mountain with a crown adorning the top, symbolizing the path toward enlightenment and Spirit.

In the upright position, Temperance is a reminder to ground oneself and find balance in all things. It also calls on the reader to remain calm and patient when pursuing anything. Not everything will come to pass when we want it to. The cups symbolize the need to stay active in this life, whether it be achieving our dreams, remaining in tune with the Universe, or finding our life's purpose. Without growth, we stagnate.

When reversed, Temperance can be a warning that you are leaning too heavily on one side of something and losing the ever-important equilibrium of your life. If there's no balance, aspects of your existence may be out of control. It has an air of impatience and a no-nonsense attitude that prevents you from seeing with an even eye.

The Devil, along with Death, is another seemingly scary and misunderstood card in tarot. This card has given others the impression that tarot as a whole is evil when it's actually meant to reflect our relationship with evil and other negative forces. The most prominent figure is Baphomet, the horned goat of Mendes, who represents duality. He is half goat, half human; has the wings of a bat despite being a land creature; has his left hand in a peace symbol; and holds a lit torch pointed toward the human on

his right. Above his head is the inverted pentagram that shows he dabbles in dark magic.

When upright, The Devil represents the negative forces at play that can easily ensnare you, whether that be addiction, temptation, lust, or rage. The opposite of Temperance, The Devil encourages us to forgo balance to lean into our most unhealthy tendencies. Upright, this card represents what will happen to us when we give in to our darker sides. If we proceed, we'll become like the people chained to Baphomet who, though they're tied, aren't truly held captive. They can leave at any time but are choosing to stay, and by doing so, they're becoming like Baphomet. In the reverse, The Devil represents an effort to free yourself from its influences. By inverting the card, the pentagram is back in its normal position, a reminder to use your magic to fight against this dark influence.

The scene of The Tower is one of terror. The tower, built on a precarious foundation, has been struck by a bolt of lightning, removing the crown that sat atop it, and has caught on fire. Because of this, everyone has jumped to their demise as a way to escape. In the sky, there are twenty-two flame flicks representing the twelve astrological signs and the ten points of the Tree of Life.

The Tower is pretty unsettling because it shows that no matter our plans for ourselves, a divine act can completely uproot everything we've worked toward regardless of who we are—indicated by the peasant and royal flinging themselves from the chaos. Though this card seems cruel, it's not completely a bad thing. There are times when what we've created has been built on lies or a shaky foundation. Continuing on that path can lead to the same destruction over time. The Tower is a sign from Spirit that some immediate and sudden change must happen or will happen in the near future.

Upright, The Tower is referring to an external change, but inverted it refers to an internal awakening that might come to a head unless you deal with it properly. When reversed, The Tower indicates resistance to change. There may be a major change that must occur for you to continue on in your life path that you're putting off out of fear. It can also symbolize inner turmoil that might cause an upheaval in the future.

17 - THE STAR

This card, like The Tower, showcases how much the Divine is involved in our lives. In The Star, there are eight stars floating above the person in the lake, representing the seven chakras, and the final, brightest star represents the person's consciousness. The figure in The Star holds two pitchers, one pouring into the lake and the other pouring onto the earth. The pitcher in their right hand represents nourishing their internal life like their intuition and emotional side. The pitcher in their left hand is pouring into the earth, which symbolizes feeding into the practical side.

In the upright position, The Star is a wonderful card that implies inner growth and prosperity through the greenery of the landscape. It also represents vulnerability and being in harmony spiritually and physically. The Star feeds into all parts to create a positive and healthy environment. It promotes inner reflection and connection with Spirit.

In the reverse position, The Star indicates someone too concerned with the material world around them instead of their inner, richer life. It can be a sign that you aren't feeding into your spiritual self and are more into shallow pursuits. It can indicate a disconnect with your deeper consciousness and can be a warning to get back on track before you lose that connection.

THE STAR.

18 - THE MOON

Teh Moon is the stuff of dreams, literally, but more specifically the subconscious. In the sky sits both the Moon and the Sun above a land divided. Below are the two towers on opposite sides of the card, and in the foreground are a dog on the left side and a wolf on the right, representing the tamer and more animalistic sides to us. In the middle is a river separating the land.

The Moon represents our subconscious and the binary forces that influence our waking lives. During the day, we may associate strongly with our tamer, sunnier side. However, in the confines of our subconscious, we may relate to the feral, deeper side that we may not always be aware of. Although it appears as though it's separated, everything in the scene of The Moon works together at different points in time.

Upright, this card refers to our dreams and intuition. At times those aspects of ourselves can provide answers and different perspectives we wouldn't have had we not searched this aspect of our personhood. It also indicates an internal battle or uncertainty. Perhaps there's something looming in the back of your mind that you have conflicting feelings about. The Moon could be a sign that you must work through your emotions before making any sudden moves.

Reversed, The Moon symbolizes confusion and instability. Instead of understanding and using these different aspects to your advantage, they might be overwhelming you, forcing you to stagnate and be ineffective.

THE MOON.

This card is one of the best to pull. The Sun represents abundance, jubilance, success, and vitality. The Sun sits high up with his rays shining across the land and below onto the tall sunflowers that symbolize the four Minor Arcana suits.
A long red and orange flag hangs down, representing celebration and vivacity.
The child with a flower crown represents joy and innocence that buoys us during a time of warmth and favor.

In the upright position, The Sun is similar to a blessing. It's an indication that good times are ahead and that the Universe is telling you to enjoy life. If you're already experiencing a good time, it's a sign to spread that happiness to others. Happiness is fleeting, but when it arrives, it's important to hold on to it for as long as you can and give it to those around you. Life is much better when we're happy, content, and successful.

Reversed, The Sun is indicative of apathy and complacency. Instead of basking in the sunshine, one feels nothing in the Sun's presence. It can indicate a complacent person who takes these easier moments for granted. It can also denote a lack of appreciation for what you do have. No matter your lot in life, there is something to be grateful for, especially when you're paying attention to it. If The Sun is pulled in reverse, it can be a sign to look around you and see what there is to delight in.

Despite its name, Judgement isn't about being judged harshly for any specific or arbitrary reason. Instead, the card represents rebirth and the chance to look inward before moving on. In the sea rest many graves occupied by several people of varying ages who've awakened from their tombs and look upward toward the angel Gabriel who calls them to Heaven. The gray of everyone's skin represents the end of their personal cycle, similar to the gray of the Hermit to signal age and wisdom. These people

have "died" and are waiting to be reborn, to strive for higher good and a higher consciousness. Gabriel represents the Divine, who shares this goal with us.

In the upright position, Judgement is a wonderful sign of second chances and ascension to a higher spiritual plane. When this card is pulled, it's a message that rebirth is on the horizon. What triggers this rebirth could be either the act of introspection or a major life event. Either way, Judgement is indicative of an imperative decision that requires all of one's life experiences to make.

In the reversed position, this card can indicate someone who is overly judgmental, to their detriment. To judge oneself or others too severely is disastrous. It seeks to tear down and not objectively and kindly use discernment to see what does and doesn't work. This position may also be indicative of jadedness, the state of being too cynical and refusing to see the positives, especially on the cusp of change.

As the final card in the Major Arcana, The World combines the symbols of The Magician and the Wheel of Fortune. Where those cards represent genesis and the way of the Universe, this card culminates as a beginning, a full cycle, an end, and the beginning of another cycle. Within the oval wreath lies someone with two wands, similar to the Magician, in their hands. They're looking backward while their feet are moving forward, demonstrating the ability to both look back and step into the future. In the corners are the zodiac signs: Aquarius, Scorpio, Leo, and Taurus. They're here to watch and guide the reader.

When upright, The World symbolizes completion and accomplishment. It shows that a season has commenced and has now ended. When applied to a particularly difficult time in your life, it can signify that you have a future to look forward to. Because of the cyclical nature of The World, this card can be a sign to close any unfinished business so that you can move on to something better.

In the reverse position, this card can represent a need for closure to get past a period of stagnation. Similar to the Wheel of Fortune, The World is a reminder that you must keep moving forward because that's the nature of being alive. Everything must begin and end eventually. If you pull this position in a reading, it can be a message to work through any loose ends and keep your gaze forward.

THE WORLD.

Minor Arcana

N ow that we've reviewed the Major Arcana portion, it's time to delve into the Minor Arcana. Instead of covering significant themes, it covers the day-to-day of your life and refers to the immediate future rather than overarching motifs. As shown in The Magician card, this half of the deck is separated into four categories: wands, cups, swords, and pentacles. Every category represents the four directions, elements, and range of emotions. Each suit is comparable to playing card decks with an ace, numbered cards ranging from two through ten, a Queen, and a King. Unlike playing cards, these suits have a Page and Knight that, when paired with the other human cards, represent an ascending level of mastery and growth.

Despite its name, the Minor Arcana will make up most of every reading, and because of their number, you can use them to precisely customize your spells to match whatever intention you have. In this chapter, you will uncover the cards' meanings and be able to use them however you see fit. Let them guide you.

The Suit of Wands

The first suit in the Minor Arcana starts off fierce. Wands are connected to the element of fire, considered to be a masculine element. Cards of this suit revolve around passion, willpower, energy, and strength. Because it's connected to fire, Wand cards are about the more feral aspects of ourselves. Fire is one of the most basic and volatile forces of nature, so these cards deal with some of the purest aspects of personhood: creativity, enthusiasm, and sexuality.

Though these are the positives of fire, the negative aspects include egotistical behavior, recklessness, and danger. These cards will remind you that fire can be contained and used for good. However, if left unchecked, it can rage on and cause destruction in your life and in your spellwork. The correlating colors for this suit are red, orange, yellow, and gold. Respectively, they represent passion and power, joy and excitement, happiness and levity, and the Sun's authority and value.

Other names for this suit are Rods, Staves, or Staffs.
The playing card deck equivalent is the suit of Clubs.

ACE OF WANDS

The Ace of Wands features a large hand holding a towering, growing wand. Because the hand appears from a cloud, it implies that this card represents the beginning of a journey. This card indicates that the Divine is offering a fresh start to new creative pursuits. The lush landscape in the background implies that this is the beginning of a fruitful endeavor.

When upright, the Ace of Wands represents beginnings and encourages following your instincts on whatever new adventure you'd like to pursue. If you've been feeling unmotivated lately, the Ace of Wands is a sign to find what motivates you and chase that. This card is one of the purest in the deck because it's all about potential. At this point, the future is yours to create if you simply take the first step.

In a spell, this card can represent the beginning for yourself or for others. You can use it to encourage someone to start that project they've been putting off or to find the pull to begin their spiritual, mental, or emotional journey toward growth.

When reversed, the card represents uncertainty. You may have creativity or willpower built up inside you, but you may not know how to manifest it. Or you may be afraid to take the next official step to begin this new journey. Another aspect is when growth is on the horizon but something is stymieing the process. In spellwork, this can represent someone who's feeling lost and unsure of their purpose.

TWO OF WANDS

This card is all about planning. The Two of Wands features someone standing with a wand in their left hand and a globe in their right. Those aspects combined indicate that someone has taken the potential and direction of the Ace of Wands but has to plan what to do with this newfound purpose. The globe symbolizes the endless potential a person has once they know exactly what they want. The other wand symbolizes the step not yet taken.

Upright, this card represents the planning stage. Nothing has been set in stone yet and there's still plenty of time to figure it out. When this card is pulled, it's a time of discovery. Think of what you want to achieve, whether it be a profound relationship, a fulfilling career, or a spiritual journey, and plan how you will attain it. In spellwork, this can represent hesitation, the anxiety right before diving into something scary, or a person who must make up their mind.

Reversed, the Two of Wands is a sign to reevaluate your goals. Perhaps you *think* you want to take a certain path for yourself, but in reality, it's someone else's dream for you. This position encourages you to take another look. Another interpretation is someone who's stuck in the planning process. They may know what they want but are stuck in a perpetual planning phase. In spellwork, you can use this to help you or someone else sort out their problems before making any significant moves.

THREE OF WANDS

This card is one of movement and progress. The card's illustration shows a person standing with three wands looking out toward the sea with three ships sailing by. This is indicative of plans that are in motion. The Two of Wands is the first step not taken, but this card represents plans that are already in motion and the initial progress. You've made your choices and sorted through your plans, and now you must have faith in them. At this point, they're out of your control.

In the upright position, this card may suggest that you can expand on your plans and adjust accordingly. Perhaps you noticed something you forgot to incorporate or need to make a change right away; this card might be a sign to make that change as soon as possible to ensure you get what you want. It can also be a time of contemplation to see what other avenues you can go down. In magic, this can represent the spell you're working on to set your plans and the Universe in motion. It can also represent travel of some kind, whether spiritual or physical.

Reversed, this card denotes that you may have intentions, but you're playing it safe and not taking the risks they require to be actualized. It might also indicate a sudden halt of plans that's out of your control. In spellwork, this can stand for blockages or emotional impositions that prevent you from moving forward as you wish.

FOUR OF WANDS

Illustrated on this card are four wands with a canopy of grapes and flora hanging from them. In the background, two happy people stand cheering as if welcoming whoever's on the other side. The picture itself is one of warmth and celebration as if it's a setup for a party. The Four of Wands encourages you to celebrate the goals and milestones you've hit along your grand plan. Some are perfectionists who would rather celebrate when the entire plan has been actualized, but it's more important to celebrate the milestones in between. Those who love and support you want to celebrate you, so celebrate with them.

When pulled, this card is a reminder to stop and enjoy the progress you've made because joy is just as important as passion and determination. It can denote that your circle of people may want to spend time with you and celebrate with you. Additionally, it can be an indicator to take a vacation with those you enjoy spending time with. In spellwork, this card can be used to bring people together or to sweeten a future homecoming.

Conversely, this card denotes a disconnect with the people in your life, whether that be because you're focused too intently on your goals or because you feel shame for not being as far along as you'd like. It can also indicate that you're not receiving the support you hoped you'd get. In your spells, this can indicate disappointment or a fracture in familial or friendship circles.

FIVE OF WANDS

Conflict is the theme for this card. The Five of Wands is illustrated with five people with five wands appearing to strike each other; however, no one has actually made contact, giving the impression that they might be fighting for the sake of it. Each person has a varying opinion and background, as indicated by their wardrobe, leading the querent to believe that their friction comes from their differences alone rather than a true disagreement on principle.

When upright, this card is a warning not to lean into anger and defensiveness, especially when there's no true cause for it. Another interpretation is that you may be competing with others to achieve the same goal, and as a result, you're caught in a tense environment. In spellwork, this card can represent conflict and a way to work through it effectively. Whether the tension is between you and others or people affecting you, it can aid you in finding a resolution.

When reversed, this card may indicate that there's a confrontation that you're avoiding. At times, evading conflict can be beneficial, especially when the other parties aren't interested in finding a solution at that time. But if a conflict *needs* to happen to resolve an issue, the Five of Wands is telling you to address it head-on. It may also signal the end of a long-standing conflict. In spellwork, you can use this position to spur the end of a fight that's gone on far too long.

SIX OF WANDS

The Six of Wands is about accomplishment and public accolades. Depicted is a horse rider with a celebratory wreath on both their head and their wand. Next to and behind them is a group of people cheering them on. This card signifies that you've either overcome a personal goal and you're getting praise for it, or you've helped others find a solution. In combination with the Five of Wands, this can signify that you ended the big conflict and are being shown appreciation.

In the upright position, the Six of Wands represents achieving all your goals and being recognized by others for it. Those people may include teachers and classmates, bosses and coworkers, or clients and constituents. Take time to savor this and take in compliments instead of rejecting them (if you have a tendency to do so). When used in spellwork, this card can represent you or someone else in this same position. Additionally, it can signify who you may want to become. It holds the essence of achievement, which is something you can attain.

In reverse, this card may denote that you feel insecure about whatever progress you've made and don't want to share it. Or maybe you have achieved a goal, but you'd rather not disclose it. Lastly, it can indicate that there's a leadership role you're hesitant to take on out of either fear or uncertainty. In spellwork, this can represent insecurity and any blockages that can stop someone from becoming the authority figure they want to be.

Going in order, the Seven of Wands is about maintaining your position after the success of the Six of Wands. Illustrated on the card is a person wielding a wand to knock back the wands of others poking upward. The more prominent a person becomes, the more people feel threatened and want to take away power or keep it for themselves. Here's the volatility of fire.

Upright, this card represents external challenges to your status. This can take the form of envious people, those who want to achieve the same success, unforeseen circumstances, and more. This card represents the stress that may come with success. No matter the anxiety you may feel, it's important to stand your ground and keep yourself going. But know that just as there were people before you, there'll be people after you. There's nothing wrong with maintaining your position, but there must also be room for others to attain similar success. People meeting you at your level doesn't automatically mean you'll lose all your achievements. In spellwork, this can represent the feisty spirit needed to stand up for oneself against the world.

Reversed, the Seven of Wands denotes emotional overwhelm. The external forces pressing against you are becoming too much for you to handle. It can also indicate a desire to back down from a fight because you don't want any more critiques or struggles. In spellwork, this can represent someone who feels powerless and afraid they'll be swept away by the actions of others.

On the surface of the card, eight wands are suspended in the air, pointing downward as if they're being shot like arrows. In the background, the sky's clear, the land's lush, and the river moves calmly, indicating that nothing will hinder the wands from making their mark. The Eight of Wands takes place after the events of the Seven of Wands. The strife is over and you've come out the other side stronger than ever. You've taken what you've learned, regained your strength, and are now ready to apply it to your next venture.

In the upright position, the Eight of Wands represents forward, energetic movement. You have successfully secured your position and now have the power and energy to direct it elsewhere. You're renewed and more focused than ever before. It can also represent incoming news or advantageous opportunities. Prepare for the next events in your life to unfold quickly. You can use this card in spellwork if you want to hasten an event or to ready yourself for the future.

In the reversed position, this card stands for a desire to stop the sudden changes occurring in your life. Perhaps you're not ready for these new shifts and want to give yourself more time, but this position reminds you that you can't stop the passage of time. Go with the flow. Conversely, it can represent unexpected, sudden postponement, specifically with travel. In a spell, it denotes a desire to stop something from happening or to quickly move past a delay.

NINE OF WANDS

The Nine of Wands reflects a battle fought and not quite won. Depicted on the card is a worn-looking person resting on the wand in their hands while looking back toward the other eight wands they've collected and proudly displayed. On their face is a look of fierce determination to keep fighting as long as necessary to become victorious. They're injured, as indicated by the wrap on their head, but that isn't stopping them from moving on to the next challenge.

Upright, this card signifies a time to rest after a long period of action. No matter how determined we are to manifest our dreams and goals, we all need time to sit back and enjoy the progress we've made up until this point. Continuous action and energy lead to burnout and that only prolongs any plans for success.

This position also encourages you to keep moving. You have all the time, experience, and drive required to make it to the finish line. In spellwork, you can use this card as a prayer for the Universe to help you to the next stage.

In reverse, this card represents the temptation to give up at the final stage of a difficult period. You may be weary and unmotivated to keep moving forward. Turning to look back at the progress you already made, you may feel like that's enough to quit. It may also signify paranoia and a general distrust of those who you feel might interfere with your plans. In spellwork, you can use this as a representation of someone who's been prevented from getting what they want.

TEN OF WANDS

The number ten represents the end of a cycle or journey just before it's completed. On the card is a person hunched over carrying a bundle of ten wands to the nearby town. This action signifies the last step before full actualization occurs. The person just needs to deliver the wands and they'll be freed of this cycle to pursue other ventures. They need strength and a final burst of willpower to push through their discomfort and manifest their goal.

In the upright position, the Ten of Wands denotes responsibility and burdens. Because you've made it so far on your journey, others may now depend on you to help them do the same. It also represents any final tasks it will take for you to complete your journey. When you get to the end, any extra tasks or challenges may feel even heavier than before, but they're necessary for victory. In spellwork, this can be used to ask for strength during the last phase of a cycle or represent someone who's taken on too much responsibility.

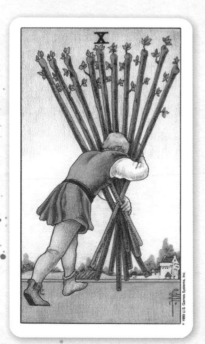

The reverse position of this card represents the weight of all your responsibilities. Instead of having the necessary strength, you're struggling to carry them all on your own. This can be a message to open up to others and delegate tasks so you can make the necessary moves for yourself. Another interpretation is to release anything that doesn't add to you accomplishing your goals. In spellwork, it denotes an overachiever who needs a break.

PAGE OF WANDS

Similar to the Ace of Wands, the Page represents an individual who's passionate and driven but lacks the experience to manifest properly. The card depicts a well-dressed youth looking up toward the wand they hold as if they're unsure of what to do with it. They're in a desert, representing how unprepared the Page is to maneuver the world around them. They have an idea of what they want but are too naive to put it into action.

Upright this card denotes a zest for life. The Page knows they're immature and wants to change that. Because of this, they strive to find new environments to learn and grow. Though inexperienced, they don't let that stop them; they know they need to go into the world, where they'll find their footing. In spellwork, this can represent a person who has the fearlessness and innocence of youth. Similar to the Fool, the Page doesn't know enough to be afraid.

Reversed, the Page is filled with too many ideas and not enough action. They have their head in the clouds so much so that they can't take the first step in any direction. On the other hand, this card can denote a person who has had many visions for themselves, but none of them ever came to fruition. As a result, they're perpetually stuck in the beginner stages. In spellwork, this can represent an immature person who needs a push to go into the real world and out of their imagination.

KNIGHT OF WANDS

The Knight is the personification of fire. The Knight rides in the desert, carries a wand, and has fire coming out of their armet, rerebrace, and couter. The cloth adorning them is shredded and gives the appearance of flames. Everything about the illustration represents action and movement. The horse is reared back with front legs in the air, ready to go full force into the next quest. On the Knight's face is a look of determination and a desire to dive headfirst into the next adventure. They won't stop for anyone but themselves.

When upright, the Knight of Wands represents the experience, desire, and willpower to accomplish whatever the Page isn't able to. The Knight follows their gut, takes charge, and doesn't ask any questions, which is helpful when you're afraid or unsure of yourself. This card encourages the reader to go with their gut and not think too hard about the consequences. In spellwork, it can represent someone impulsive and bold who wants to go, go, go without being held back.

When reversed, this card symbolizes impulsive action without any thought behind it. It's acting when inspiration strikes but with no buildup. It's fully giving in to your passions and nothing else. It can also represent someone who desires to change something about themselves or their circumstances but is unable to. In spellwork, this can represent someone who is stubbornly trying to go their own way without any outside counsel. They're only listening to themselves, but to their detriment.

KNIGHT of WANDS.

QUEEN OF WANDS

The Queen of Wands is a boss. Period. She is comfortable and confident in her role as Queen. She sits on her throne in between the sand dunes and the white of winter as if she straddles the heat and passion of fire as well as the cool collectedness of ice. She wears a yellow dress accompanied by the sunflower in her left hand and the sunflowers etched into her throne to symbolize life and joy. Before her is an adorable black cat that gives the impression she is into occult magic as well.

When upright, the Queen symbolizes a trusted leader and manager. The Queen knows who she is and her charisma and status encourage others to do better. She's a master delegator and knows how to incorporate the talent and knowledge of the people around her. As a leader, she's excellent with teamwork. In spellwork, she represents a beloved female authority figure who exudes confidence and self-assuredness.

When reversed, the Queen symbolizes a person who isn't as well liked but who's also not interested in the opinions of others. They go their own way and are proudly doing so without caring about what anyone thinks. It can also represent someone who isn't as confident as the Queen but who is instead insecure and perhaps a little quieter. In spellwork, this can represent someone in authority who may not be an ideal leader or someone who hasn't found their footing in a leadership role.

KING OF WANDS

The King, similar to the Queen, is a charming leader who has people at their disposal. Unlike the Queen, the King of Wands is more interested in using others to see his plans come to fruition. He has expansive ideas and desires and will use those around him to make them happen. He is the classic idea of a king, adorned with a cape that features salamanders eating their tails as a sign of infinity. The King sits on his throne looking onward, signifying his long-term visions for himself.

In the upright position, the King denotes stepping into a highly visible leadership role. He represents a person who knows exactly what he wants to accomplish and what needs to be done to actualize it. His singular mindset attracts others who share similar goals and desires, while his maturity gives people confidence that they can achieve anything. In spellwork, this can represent what you want to be as a leader yourself or an authority figure in your real life that you admire.

In the reverse position, the King represents someone who may set unrealistic expectations of themselves or the people tasked to help them. This can devolve into arrogance and force others to stick with their vision without listening to input. The King can also show you what you're meant to be but aren't ready to be. In spellwork, this can represent an insecure leader who lacks the wisdom and personality to lead effectively.

The Suit of Cups

Similar to Wands, the Suit of Cups centers on emotions, but where Wands' emotion focuses more on the self, Cups are about how we feel about ourselves and others. Water is the element of Cups, a gentler force than fire; however, water has its duality. It can be still and gentle, but also wild and rageful. Instead of dealing with what's in the mind, this suit deals with what's in the heart.

Seasonally, the Suit of Cups is associated with summer, a time of abundance and harvest. When pulled during a reading, Cup cards tell you to examine or follow your emotions wherever they lead. In spellwork, they can be used for matters of the heart, intuition, relationships, and inner consciousness. This suit is as versatile as water itself. Cups are linked to creativity, imagination, and love. On water's more dangerous side, Cups may signify an inability to express oneself, a lack of creativity and logic, and being overly absorbed in one's emotions.

Another name for Cups is Chalices and it represents Hearts in playing card decks.

Pictured on the Ace of Cups is a hand, representing the Divine, appearing from the clouds holding a golden cup. From the cup spring five streams of water, which flow into a lake of lilies that represent life. Atop the cup is a dove, symbolizing God, paused mid-flight, placing a wafer with a cross on it into the chalice. It's an image teeming with life and divinity, showing that emotions are inherently spiritual and a part of being alive. The hand offering the full chalice encourages you to drink from it, to give in to your emotions.

The Ace of Cups is a sign from the Universe that it's time to open your heart. It's a card of new beginnings that requires you to be open to new relationships that will come your way. It's a refreshing start to a new pairing, whether that be a friendship, a mentorship, or a romantic relationship. When pulled upright in a reading, it's an indication to dive deep into your emotions and let them fortify you.

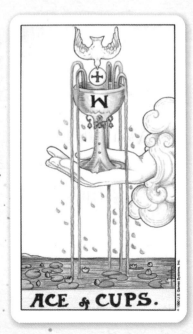

When reversed, this card may be a sign that you are suppressing your emotions. Instead of responding to the call of the Divine, you're choosing to ignore its encouragement. This may come from pain or fear of being vulnerable. It can also symbolize emptiness. From this position, water completely falls out of the cup, leaving nothing behind. When used in spellwork, this card can signify a blockage in your spirit, preventing you from accessing your inner consciousness.

TWO OF CUPS

Illustrated on this card are two people each holding a cup while making eye contact. The person on the right reaches for the person on the left's hand as if they're trying to establish a connection. Above the cups is the symbol of Hermes's caduceus; it's often related to commerce, negotiation, trade, proper conduct, and protection. Above that is a red chimera that represents passion and, depending on the relationship, sexual energy. Combined, these symbols represent two people who are coming together to form a new relationship. It's a positive symbol of new beginnings and initial mutual trust.

When upright, this card denotes a mutual understanding between two people and the caduceus contextualizes the relationship. It may be a friendship, mentorship, business relationship, or romantic relationship. Regardless, this card represents the initial connection between two people based on attraction, respect, or similar values—possibly all three. This card can be used in spellwork to represent the kind of relationship you may want for yourself or others.

When reversed, this card denotes an unhealthy attachment to another person. Instead of two individuals connecting on mutual goals and interests, one may be more interested in the idea of another person and not who they actually are, creating a toxic relationship. It may also indicate a relation that was once beneficial but is now unequal and draining. In spellwork, this card can be used to dissolve a connection that no longer has any value or is actively harming both parties.

THREE OF CUPS

The spirit of the Three of Cups is summarized in one word: Hooray! Three people stand with their cups in the air as if in celebration of their relationships with each other. They dance with fruits and vegetables at their feet, symbolizing abundance and vitality. In complete communion, this trio is bound by camaraderie and a joint effort toward a mutual goal. They can represent dear friends, family, work relations, or even hobbyist groups connected by the same wishes. The Three of Cups is a celebratory card that's all about uplifting yourself and others around you.

When upright, this card signifies siblinghood and a desire to be around others you're deeply connected to. If pulled in a reading, it can be a sign to schedule a day or night out with your inner circle. Doing so will fortify your soul and ultimately make you happy. It's an extremely positive and wholesome card. In a spell, it can be used to foster friendships with others who love you and have similar mindsets to you.

When reversed, this card denotes a disconnect from your inner circle. Something is holding you back from spending time with these people. You may not be able to spare the time from other obligations or you may be going through a period of illness that prevents you from being around others. In spellwork, you can use this card to shatter the barrier between you and others, whether that be miscommunication or a busy schedule.

FOUR OF CUPS

This card features a person sitting atop a small hill with their arms and legs crossed. Before them sit three cups in a row while another cup is being offered to them from the Divine. Their pose doesn't quite match the world around them. They sit beneath a shaded tree on a clear day surrounded by lush grass and healthy trees in the distance. This pose denotes being closed off from the surrounding environment to the point where a gift from the Universe goes completely unnoticed.

In the upright position, the Four of Cups is indicative of apathy and ignorance. The person on the card is too in their own head, either because of overthinking or meditating, to notice another opportunity from the Divine to gain more creativity or perspective. It may also indicate that you're focusing more on what's already in front of you than on what new things are coming your way. Another interpretation is an overall disinterest in delving deeper into your inner consciousness. In spellwork, this can be used if you want the Universe to inspire you.

When reversed, this card encourages looking inward to sort yourself out to then be open to a new level of emotional intimacy. It may denote that you're coming out of an indifferent state and into a deeper understanding that life is beautiful and something you need to participate in. When used in spellwork, this can represent a person who's withdrawn and needs a push from the Divine to get out of this state.

FIVE OF CUPS

This card depicts a lone figure in black standing between three overturned cups before them and two upright cups behind them. Their posture and cloak denote a time of mourning over the overturned cups. What was once in them has now been absorbed into the ground, robbing the figure of any previous progress made. Not all hope is lost because there are still two cups that are perfectly fine, but the figure is too preoccupied with loss to notice. The land is split by a raging river separating the figure from home; it shows how overwhelming emotion can cloud someone's judgment.

In the upright position, the Five of Cups symbolizes disappointment and regret—two emotions that can linger if you let them—and the result of staying in the past and refusing to move on. The sky is cloudy as if the entire environment is responding to the figure's mood. Though it's normal to be upset, rageful, or regretful, remaining in that state can stagnate any possible growth or happiness you can feel, as indicated by the cups behind the figure. Such a state stymies maturity.

Reversed, this card shows significant recovery from debilitating feelings. It's a reminder that you can't alter the past or what has hurt you. Instead, you must focus on the gifts you've been given and learn to let go of what you've lost. No matter what stage you're in in your life, there is truly always something to be appreciative of. In spellwork, this can be used to trigger healing.

SIX OF CUPS

What separates this card from the others is the childlike veneer that touches every detail in the illustration. The roofs of the buildings have a shine to them as if they've been polished. The two children featured on the card look chipper and kind, with the taller child handing over a cup with a white flower in it to the smaller child. In this card, each cup has its own flower in it, signifying innocence.

In the upright position, this card is about childhood memories, specifically cherished ones. Everything in this card denotes a positive memory, such as sharing, the bloom of life, and being safe in a secure area. For many, childhood is a time when the world didn't seem so scary. It's also a time when many of us were our truest selves. That time is the foundation that carries us into adulthood. This card encourages the reader to use a past memory to affect or inform the future. In spellwork, this can be the catalyst for manifestation. Positive memories can be just as effective as negative ones.

In the reverse, this card signifies that you're clinging too much to the past as a way to not deal with the present. Where the Five of Cups clings to regret, the Six of Cups clings to an idealized past that may not have been as lovely as you remember. Instead of using the past as a catapult, you're using it as an excuse to not move forward.

SEVEN OF CUPS

The Seven of Cups is the card for fantasizers. On it stands a shadowed figure looking upon seven golden cups resting atop a cloud, like in a dream. Though all the cups look shiny and new, if someone were to take a step closer, they'd see each one carries its own contents, representing different realities. From the top left to right a cup holds a human head, a robed figure, then a snake. From the bottom left to right, a cup holds a castle, riches, a wreath, and a dragon. Each choice seems exciting and too good to be true, but the message of this card is to think before acting on impulse. Not everything is what it appears to be.

When upright, this card is a warning against keeping your head in the clouds and not in reality. Every cup has its advantages and disadvantages, but all that can be seen is what breaches the rim of the cup. So picking one seemingly favorable cup may have

unfortunate consequences when applied to reality. Anything sounds wonderful in dreams, but reality often corrects us. In spellwork, this can be used as a way to avoid this type of thinking and bring someone back down to earth.

When reversed, this card represents a thoughtful person willing to take a step back and analyze their many choices. They can recognize when they're fantasizing and are aware enough to see through the illusions. In spells, use this card to denote wisdom and control.

EIGHT OF CUPS

Like the Five of Cups, this card is about disappointment and dissatisfaction. Unlike that card, the figure in the Eight of Cups is making a physical attempt to move on. In this card, a caped figure with a walking stick is walking away from their stack of eight cups on their way to new beginnings. Their cups are stacked in a way that indicates incompletion, as if there would have been a ninth, but the figure gave up. They take their leave during the night, as indicated by the Moon above and the shadows over the land.

Upright, this card represents unhappiness at what life currently has to offer. It can indicate that someone may have created a path for themselves over time but are no longer fulfilled by it. This path can take the form of a job, a relationship, or an incompatible friend group. The cups they've left behind are indicative of emotional attachments. By leaving suddenly, the figure acts as though they don't exist and is trying to separate themselves from their past. In spellwork, this can be used to leave a harmful situation for a better life.

Reversed, this card encourages waiting a moment before making a decision. Instead of making sudden moves, you're gently being told to weigh your options and determine what's truly best for you. In spellwork, this can be used to spur you or someone else to gather the courage to make the best choice toward happiness and contentment.

As the ninth card in the deck, the Nine of Cups represents the tail end of a journey. In combination with the Eight of Cups, this card suggests that you or someone else has made their life choices and is now content with them. On the card sits a figure on a wooden bench with arms crossed and a satisfied smile on their face. Behind them is a high shelf covered in a light blue cloth with nine cups lined up in a neat row. The cloth represents the stillness of life and emotions. It gives the impression of a calm waterfall.

In the upright position, this card is immensely positive. It represents emotional and spiritual satisfaction with life, accomplishments, and even material possessions. If this isn't an accurate reflection of life, the Nine of Cups is a harbinger of good to come. Another interpretation is that this card is an encouragement

to celebrate life, whether that means enjoying what life has already given you or what you have yet to experience. In spellwork, along with tangible action, this card can be used as a wish to the Universe so you can reach fulfillment.

Reversed, this card signifies a shallow satisfaction. The Nine of Cups can indicate that you may have the appearance of a good life, but really you feel hollow inside. It suggests that you may be chasing what others think your life should be and not necessarily what you want for yourself.

TEN OF CUPS

The numbered Cups cards end harmoniously with the Ten of Cups. This card represents love and connection between you and your inner circle. In the sky is an arc of cups within a rainbow. Below that stand a couple holding each other while their children dance and play together. In the background there is a calm river and the couple's house on a hill. Everything is peaceful.

Upright, this card indicates emotional fulfillment in all relations: romantic, familial, and with the overall community. If you don't have a romantic partner, this card is a sign that you will have one in time if you so desire. However, if you are in a relationship, this card suggests you may want to or will start having children soon. But overall, this card represents being in harmony with all your relationships. The Ten of Cups indicates a time of joy and contentment. In spellwork, you can use this as a blessing for yourself or others.

Reversed, this card means you may not feel connected to your inner circle. Perhaps you haven't seen them in a while because life's gotten in the way or perhaps you've been struggling to find common ground as a result of personal growth or life changes. This card indicates the need to reach out and be present with those in your life. In spellwork, use this position to open the hearts of those you seek emotional intimacy with. That and tangible efforts on your part can manifest your desires.

PAGE OF CUPS

PAGE of CUPS.

Featured on this card is the Page standing on the shore of an active ocean. They've also donned a blue tunic printed with blooming flowers. With a smile on their face, the Page looks at the fish inside their cup in a relaxed and pleased pose. The Page represents someone full of potential. The fish in the cup represents a sudden new idea or inspiration. All that's left for the Page is to choose where to funnel their time and energy.

Upright, this card represents a time of serendipity where you're struck with an indication to do more with your emotions, creativity, or intuition. The Page can denote seeking emotionally fulfilling activities like volunteering or meditation. Take whatever inspiration strikes you and run with it: start a photography class, learn to forage, or deepen your psychic abilities. In spellwork, this may be a message to take your potential and channel it into something profound.

Reversed, the Page may indicate a creative block. You may want to break into a new creative endeavor but don't have faith in yourself to actually do it. Your inner saboteur may tell you that you don't have the talent and you're taking it to heart. In spellwork, this card can represent that saboteur and you can use this card to banish it. Alternatively, you may be hiding your creative pursuits for fear of judgment. This position encourages you to share because you may inspire others and vice versa.

KNIGHT OF CUPS

The Knight struts across the arid land. Unlike in other Knight cards, the Knight moves steadily in no rush. In the Knight's hand, they hold a golden cup outward, signaling they have a firm grip on their emotions. On their body is a cloth printed with fish, representing water, and on their head and feet are wings, denoting forward motion. This Knight listens to their heart and follows it relentlessly, whether or not it abides by any logic. They are the ultimate romantic who is in touch with their emotions and isn't ashamed of them.

Where the Page is focused on where to funnel their inspiration, the Knight in the upright position is focused on turning their emotions into action. They take their emotions and use them toward creating beauty, attracting others, and generally trying to better the world around them. They're the light in the room and wear their heart on their sleeve. You may use this card in a love spell to attract a person like this.

In reverse, this card might mean you're following your heart so much that you've now become moody. Though the heart can be true, it's also ruled by emotions that rise and fall depending on outer and inner circumstances. Because of this, you're being held back from performing any action or forward movement. In spellwork, this can represent someone who's so caught up in their emotional world they've lost touch with reality and may need a push in the right direction.

QUEEN OF CUPS

The Queen is the calm ruler of her emotions. She resides on the shore before the swirling ocean. Peppered under her feet are various seashells and colorful sea glass. The Queen holds an elaborate golden chalice with angels on the sides, signifying divine intuition. The chalice indicates the Queen's emotions come from deep within her soul. Her throne sitting near, but not in, the sea shows that she feels her emotions but isn't overwhelmed by them.

In the upright position, the Queen represents someone who is emotionally mature, compassionate, and sensitive to other people's feelings. She listens to others and gives them the space to express themselves without letting their feelings alter her own. It may indicate someone who has a trustworthy intuition. This may denote your higher self or someone you aspire to be. In spellwork, this can be used to connect to divine intuition and the feelings of others you may not understand. Or it can be used to connect to the Moon to manifest some of your desires.

In the reverse position, the Queen represents someone who may be giving too much to others and not enough to themselves. This may also indicate a codependent relationship. As a result, you're no longer in tune with your own emotions but instead are meshing yourself with someone else. In spellwork, this card can be used as a first step in pulling away from others and finding inner balance once again.

KING OF CUPS

The patriarch of the court cards, the King sits on his throne on the sea itself. Despite the busy traffic of the ocean—the fish to his right and the ship to his left—he is calm and in control of his emotions. In one hand he holds a cup and in the other a scepter, indicating that he's in tune with his inner self but also clear-headed and logical. Instead of looking at his cup, he looks off into the distance, showing that he is aware of his feelings, but is not necessarily ruled by them.

Upright, the King denotes an emotionally stable and mature person; this could represent you or someone else. The King is someone who, when faced with adversity, doesn't immediately give in to despair. Instead, he knows to rein in his temper and his reactions and then move forward with a clear mind. The King is compassionate and wise. He's willing to offer advice and emotional support to anyone who needs it. In spellwork, this can represent a fatherly figure, a teacher, or a mentor.

Reversed, this card signifies a King who's unstable and controlling. Rather than offering advice, the King manipulates the feelings of others to do his bidding. In this position, the King represents someone who gives in to their emotions and then feeds off drama and chaos. Order and calm bore him, so he tries to create situations that foster discomfort and confrontation. In spellwork, this card can represent a toxic person, but especially a toxic person in power.

The Suit of Swords

Out of all the suits, the Suit of Swords is the most logical. It deals with the element of air, which is clear, swift, and decisive. Within tarot, air represents logic, intellect, and power. Combined with Swords, air represents using the mind to decipher your next course of action.

Swords on their own have two edges, meaning they can be used for good and for evil. On one hand, they can be used to sever, make quick decisions, and as an empowering tool. On the other hand, swords can be used to attack brashly and hurt others, intentionally or not.

Unlike previous suits, Swords, though more analytical, are also more tragic. Many of the cards involve heartbreak, stress, betrayal, and feeling trapped despite moving about with cultivated intelligence. Swords, because they're predominantly used as a weapon of offense, are naturally a cause of conflict. There's a delicate balance to using swords, and it's important to be aware of it, otherwise it can cause damage that's difficult to undo.

In a playing card deck, Swords are the equivalent of Spades.

ACE OF SWORDS

Illustrated on the Ace of Swords is a hand appearing from a cloud, representing the Divine, holding a gleaming sword. Atop the sword is a crown and wreaths. Combined, these elements represent conquering any obstacle with logic and reasoning and coming out on top. In the background, there are jagged mountains and bare terrain, indicating that the road ahead is going to be arduous. But with your sword, you can handle all deterrents.

Upright, the Ace of Swords represents a breakthrough way of thinking. Perhaps you've been in a rut and haven't managed to get out of it. This card is a sign that the rut will end and you'll be struck with a different perspective. When this card is pulled, it's a sign to start a new project you haven't had the mindset to do before. In spellwork, you can use this to either hasten inspiration or use it as a way to find a new perspective to manifest goals.

When reversed, this card indicates that you may be stubbornly holding on to a certain way of thinking in order to achieve your goals, but that thinking isn't helpful. In this position, the card is telling you to review your current mindset and see whether there's another way you can tackle your goals that's more effective. In spellwork, use this to break mental chaos and confusion for yourself or others. The Ace of Swords can aid you in breaking this useless cycle and moving on toward something practical and effective.

Confusion is the theme of the Two of Swords. Illustrated on the card is a masked person with their arms crossed, resting identical swords on their shoulders. Each sword is identical in both appearance and length. This means that the blindfolded person has two similar choices that they need to make, but they are unsure which one to choose. They're sitting on a stone bench momentarily until they can decide what to do. Behind them is an open sea peppered with rocks, potentially signifying a difficult path and choice. In the upper right corner of the card sits a crescent Moon that indicates following their intuition.

When upright, the Two of Swords represents confusion or hesitation. The blindfolded figure isn't able to fully understand or see all the options available to them. They aren't informed enough to make a decision one way or another. A similar interpretation is that the figure wants to be impartial and doesn't want to know the additional details for fear that will cloud their judgment. In spellwork, this can represent an indecisive person who must make a decision immediately.

Reversed, this card denotes having so much information between the two decisions that you're immobilized. The weight of the choices may be so overwhelming that you feel as though a decision *can't* be made; you're frozen in place. Alternatively, the two swords represent two people coming to blows and you're trapped in the middle, unsure of how to help. In spells, this card dispels conflict and quickens resolution.

THREE OF SWORDS

Gloom permeates the Three of Swords. In the foreground, a bright red heart has been pierced with three swords. Behind it the sky is gray and it's raining, reflecting the mood of the card. Every aspect represents the pain and sadness that comes from negative thoughts, cruel words, and betrayal. This card reflects one of the lowest points in a person's life.

When upright, the Three of Swords denotes literal heartbreak that comes from others' actions. It represents a time of grief and loss. The unbridled pain that comes from heartbreak is something everyone must experience; it's a part of life. This card also represents emotional release. There are times when we want to be strong, so we shove our feelings down and refuse to face them. When anguish of this caliber comes into our lives, it can force us to express the feelings we've bottled up. You may use this in spells to harness your pain and convert it into powerful magic to manifest another goal.

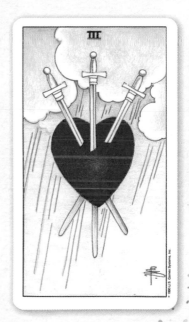

When reversed, this card can reflect that you're in a particularly vulnerable position. You may have just gone through a period of profound sadness and are an open wound. This card's telling you that you should begin healing. Grief can't last forever. You'll see the other side. This position reminds you that it'll take some time, but it is possible. In spellwork, this can be used to heal a broken heart with the faith that things will get better.

After the anguish of the Three of Swords, the Four of Swords is about a period of rest—no more pain or strife, only slumber. At the bottom of the card sits a golden tomb with a carving of a knight atop the lid. They have their eyes closed and their hands folded together as if in prayer. Below the knight is a golden sword that represents the knight's will to fight. It's been laid to rest, no longer prepared for conflict. Above them rest three swords pointing at the knight's head, heart, and torso. These represent the mental, emotional, and physical attacks the knight endured in life. In the upper left corner is a stained-glass window, depicting another adult and child, highlighting the good the knight has experienced.

Upright, this card signifies resting, especially after a period of discord. After being on edge, it's time to relax and engage in silent contemplation. This card also indicates a forced period of rest, such as planning a vacation or time off. You must rest before moving on to the next challenge. Use this card in spellwork to get yourself in the mood to relax.

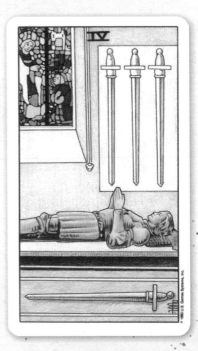

Reversed, this card denotes restlessness. Perhaps you want to rest but you haven't been given the chance to, so you've pushed yourself relentlessly, hurtling yourself toward burnout. It's a warning that if you *don't* rest, you'll be out of commission whether you want to be or not. In spellwork, this can represent someone who refuses to quit but needs to.

FIVE OF SWORDS

Moving on from the previous card, the Five of Swords represents an intense conflict that's now been won. The victor, the figure in the foreground with the smug smirk, is collecting the swords that were used in battle. Behind the victor are their two opponents, both walking away in shame. Based on their postures, they've failed in front of an entire audience. Though the fight is over, there's bitterness in the air, as indicated by the dark clouds in an otherwise clear day.

In the upright position, this card represents conflict and

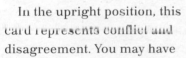

disagreement. You may have had a fierce falling-out with someone—a spouse, partner, family member, coworker, classmate—and even though the fight has ended, there are still hard feelings. One or both of you may have been more concerned with being "right" than considering the other's point of view, resulting in bad blood. Winning truly isn't everything, especially in interpersonal relationships. In spellwork, this can be used to help you calm down enough to see reason and not be clouded by your pride.

Reversed, the card can indicate you want to end a conflict because you see no value in continuing, but the other person won't let go. This person's inability to move on prohibits you from moving on, further cementing you in a place that you don't even want to be in. The presence of swords means you must be defensive even though you simply want to lay them down. In spellwork, use this card as a way to sever the conflict indefinitely.

The Six of Swords is a card of transition. In the rowboat sits a parent and child huddled close together. Because the parent wears a shroud, it alludes to the possibility that they don't want to be identified. Their previous life may have been dangerous or toxic and they recognize that they need to leave. On the bow of the boat stand six swords representing the knowledge and baggage the family will take with them toward their new home. The water to the right of the boat is turbulent, but the water toward the new land is serene, implying things will get better.

When upright, this card signifies letting go of past trauma and taking the wisdom and knowledge needed to move on. While you're going through the transition, take the time to sort through your thoughts and feelings so that you can be better prepared for the future. Use this card in spells that involve adjusting to new situations and environments.

In reverse, this card denotes a resistance to change. You may know exactly what you need to do to flee a bad situation, but you may be unable to do so because you're still attached somehow or because it's not safe yet. This card is a gentle reminder that no matter when or how, you must leave the current harmful situation or environment. In spellwork, use this card as a way to gather strength and the courage to transition for your own betterment.

Depicted on this card is a sneaky thief stealing swords from a nearby military camp. The thief has their arms full with five swords and left two behind. In the distance on the left-hand side of the card is a small group of soldiers who have seemingly caught the thief in the act. One soldier lifts a weapon in the air as if the group is about to charge forward, yet the thief is confident that they'll get away with it.

Upright, the Seven of Swords denotes deception, disgrace, and interference. This card is a warning to be aware of those in your life who may deceive you or try to take from you. Perhaps this person is a scammer, a friend of a friend, or even someone you trust. The Seven of Swords isn't meant to make you paranoid; rather, it wants you to listen to your intuition and protect yourself from those who may want to hurt you. In spellwork, use this card

in a protection spell to ward off any tricksters. Pair this with a King or Queen card for extra influence in your spell.

Reversed, this card encourages you to look inward; you're the one deceiving others. Perhaps you have a deep secret you're keeping from others because you know releasing this information will cause conflict. Or perhaps you're hiding an inner truth to your own detriment. In spellwork, this can be used to gather the courage to share the secret with others and free yourself.

EIGHT OF SWORDS

The theme of this card is despair. Illustrated on this card is a person tied up and blindfolded standing amid swords that ensnare them in place. The sky is gray, mirroring feelings of hopelessness and entrapment. Though all hope may seem lost, if the figure were to fight against their binds and remove their blindfold, they'd see that they can easily escape. They have one foot on land and the other in the water, signifying that they're confused whether or not to trust their senses or their intuition.

In the upright position, this card represents a victim mentality. This isn't to say that you aren't in an awful situation, but you may believe you can't escape it, that you're incapable of changing it. But like the figure on the card, all you have to do is find the bravery and confidence to remove your blindfold and find freedom. Pair this card with the Knight of Swords to petition the Universe to show you a way out of the predicament you're in.

In reverse, the Eight of Swords denotes that you are on the cusp of breaking free of self-imposed limitations. You're close to a breakthrough and are beginning to see that not all mental and emotional limits are insurmountable. No matter who you are, there are bound to be some bouts of self-talk that prevent you from reaching your full potential. Use this card to petition the Universe to give you the mindset you need to be free.

NINE OF SWORDS

Exemplified on the Nine of Swords is someone who has seemingly woken up from a nightmare. Their posture suggests a sudden awakening and transition from dream to harsh reality. Carved on the side of the figure's bed is a depiction of a sword fight mid-defeat. Beside the figure is a wall covered in swords representing the anxious thoughts they're carrying with them even while asleep. Covering their lap is a blanket printed with roses and all the astrological signs. The blanket represents the need for self love, especially during times of mental anguish.

Upright, this card represents constant worry and stress. One or multiple things are constantly on your mind and they're inescapable. The black wall represents the abyss that colors a mental spiral. When pulled, this card is telling you that your anguish is mental and not necessarily a reflection of reality. Though painful, there's hope you can get over this difficult period. Use this card in release spells. Pair it with the Three of Swords to encourage a good cry before resting up with the Four of Swords.

Reversed, this card is encouraging you to share your concerns with someone. That person may be a friend, a parent, or a mental health professional—anyone you can confide in. This position indicates the need to share your fears with someone so you can get a reality check on your perspective. Someone else may be able to show you that your fears are surmountable. Use this card to remind yourself to open up.

The Ten of Swords represents the lowest point of a person's life. Depicted is a person face down on the ground with ten swords that have been stabbed into them. Blood seeps from their body. The air is still and the sky is shrouded in black and clouds, reflecting the somber nature of death. Yet, despite this, the Sun is rising on the horizon. All will be well in time.

In the upright position, this card depicts an epic tragedy. The swords sticking out of the figure can represent harmful thoughts, past hurts, emotional baggage, or severe betrayal. It's the point when you feel as though everything is against you and you have no fight left in you. Times like these are the most draining and painful you can imagine. But despite this, the Ten of Swords is reminding you that, even at this low point, the Sun will rise again and you will heal. Use this card as a reminder that this is the end of one cycle but not all.

Reversed, this card represents rock bottom but is also a symbol of hope. This is as low as you will go. Nothing can get worse than this, which means there's nowhere else to go but up. This card's message isn't telling you to hurry and feel better, but is actually letting you know you can only improve from here. Carry this card with you during a particularly hard time as a reminder to let go of your pain.

PAGE OF SWORDS

On a mossy rock precipice stands the Page, gripping a sword and facing the wind. Everything's moving in this card: the wind, the clouds, the Page's hair, and the waves in the background. The Page represents a maverick who has plenty of ideas that they want to and will execute. They have all the confidence in the world to act on their ideas and imagination. On their face is a look of determination and conquest. The Page believes they can and will change the world.

Upright, the Page denotes someone faced with a new challenge, perhaps in a new environment with strangers. The Page is someone who believes in themselves and their ideas. They know they have something to offer and aren't afraid to speak their mind. Despite their age, they believe they have a fresh perspective and valuable insight to share. Because they have the wind on their side, they are emboldened in everything they do. Use this card in spellwork as inspiration to give yourself the same confidence the Page possesses.

Reversed, the Page represents someone who is arrogant and too brash with their words. They don't listen to others, nor do they value any dissenting opinions. Instead, they'd much rather hear themselves talk and not listen to those around them. Confidence turns into arrogance and fresh perspectives turn into uninformed opinions. In spellwork, use this card to remind yourself that the Page has as many edges as their sword. Be aware of them and remain levelheaded.

KNIGHT OF SWORDS

Dashing through the land, the Knight of Swords charges through the air with their sword lifted high, dressed in red, letting fierce determination guide them forward. Gales distort the clouds and nearly rip the trees from their roots, but the Knight doesn't care. In fact, the forceful winds spur the Knight on to complete his intended mission regardless of the danger. The red on his armor represents passion and conflict, as if the Knight knows they'll get into a verbal or mental battle.

In the upright position, the Knight signifies someone who has an idea in their head and will stop at nothing to implement it. Unlike the Page, the Knight has the physical means to quickly put their ideas into motion. This access and fortification allow the Knight to barrel through anyone and anything in order to manifest their desires. They disregard consequences and are single-mindedly driven. In spellwork, use this card when you need to jump into a new venture before you have time to psych yourself out.

In reverse, the Knight denotes someone with all the energy to achieve anything, but not any specific direction they want to channel it into. They're the equivalent of a rebel without a cause. Without any actual direction, they're particularly dangerous. People with energy but too much time tend to be more destructive. Use this card in spells if you know a Knight and want to get them to slow down and consider where to put their time and effort.

Atop her stone throne sits the Queen of Swords. In her right hand she steadily holds her sword, and in her left, she reaches her palm out as if asking others to come to her with their questions. Don't misunderstand the look on her face. The Queen may seem strict, but she has compassion for others, as indicated by the cherubs on the sides of her throne. Butterflies appear alongside the cherubs as well as make up her crown. They represent transformation and beauty.

Upright, the Queen represents relying on logic rather than emotions when making decisions. The Queen is wise enough that she has a solid sense of what's based in truth and what's based in emotion, but she's also open to hearing differing perspectives. Women are often talked over or ignored for their opinions, but the Queen is a reminder to stick to what you know is right and be fair with your judgments. In spellwork, when you are unsure of yourself, use the Queen to help guide you to making the right choice.

Reversed, this card represents someone who is using their heart more than their mind. When not functioning in reality, fake, exaggerated scenarios can pop into the mind to create a situation that doesn't exist. This can lead to misunderstandings that then result in poor judgment. If you know you're too deep in your feelings, use this card to remind yourself to think logically, separated from internal turmoil.

The King of Swords is the epitome of intellect within the Sword cards. Being the patriarch of the court cards, he has superb intelligence and superior counsel. Unlike the Queen, the King is much sterner and carries himself as the authority figure he is. Unlike the other court cards, there are no wild winds here. The King sits comfortably in a calm spot, giving the impression of stability.

In the upright position, the King suggests being firm in any major decision you must make. The King doesn't bow or bend to anyone. When pulled in a reading, this may be a sign to speak your truth and enforce any boundaries you must uphold. Carry yourself like the royal that you are and don't let those who have no power over you force you to waver. In spellwork, use the King to fortify your convictions. If you know you need to enforce a rule, channel the King's fearlessness into you.

In the reverse position, this card can represent someone who abuses their authority to quell the opinions of others in favor of their own. The King in this position is more tyrannical and uninterested in being fair or logical and is instead using rules or the law against others but for himself. This position can also indicate someone who believes they're intelligent, but they aren't. Rather, they see themselves as a King when really, they're a Fool. In spellwork, use this card to bind someone who's acting similarly to the reversed King.

The Suit of Pentacles

The final suit in the tarot is the Suit of Pentacles. Where other suits deal with emotions, Pentacles deal with material possessions and physical health. Aside from wellness, Pentacles predominantly represent external concepts like stability, security, wealth, and prosperity. Because these concepts are external and somewhat in our control, we have to actively work toward health, security, and stability.

Earth is the element of Pentacles, meaning these cards deal with the foundations on which we all live, but also the ups and downs of life. The Earth has a predictable four seasons and the cards will remind you to be flexible to change. Know that all the concepts surrounding Pentacles will fluctuate over time.

The downsides of Pentacles are greed, possessiveness, and an inability to adapt to change. These can cause a person to become too involved in the material world to the point that they ignore emotional or logical pursuits. Everything Pentacles represent is important, but it's also imperative to maintain balance.

The playing card equivalent is Diamonds.

ACE OF PENTACLES

Featured on the card is a shining hand extending from a cloud holding a giant pentacle. Below the hand is a rich, lush land with white lilies, vibrant grass, and a colorful archway teeming with flora. Behind that are tall blue mountains, representing hard work and intuition. The time to act is now; a path is laid out for you.

In the upright position, the Ace of Pentacles represents a moment of luck. When this appears, it's a message telling you that now is the time to start a new venture that will result in greater health and wealth. This represents the beginning of any planned goals. The Universe is sending the message that you'll be blessed with whatever ambition you choose to pursue. In spellwork, you can use this to petition the Universe to show you when you can put your plans into action.

In the reversed position, this card indicates a bad investment. If you've been wondering whether or not to invest in something, the Ace of Pentacles is letting you know not to. Instead of an opportune moment, it's a situation to be avoided. In fact, it's also a message to be careful with your spending. There may be an unexpected cost that you'll need to pay and you'll be happy you didn't spend carelessly. In spellwork, use this card to ward off any scams or inopportune moments that might worsen your financial situation. If you can avoid those moments, it will benefit your mental and emotional health.

L ike the number two itself, the Two of Pentacles is about balance; every aspect of the card reflects this. The person on the card is balancing two pentacles in their hands within the infinity symbol. Additionally, they're standing on one foot while also wearing a heavy, pointed hat that may be throwing them off. In the background there are two ships sailing on the rough, fluctuating waves, symbolizing the need for control in order to navigate difficult situations.

When upright, the Two of Pentacles denotes that you're currently balancing a lot and you're doing it well. It may not be easy, but you're successful. The Two of Pentacles can indicate that there are two major concerns you're balancing. It could be your career and your love life or your family life and friendships. Because the figure is already struggling to balance two, this card suggests not adding anything more to your plate in fear of losing balance and facing

negative consequences. Use this card in spellwork when you're striving to achieve equilibrium in your life but it's proving difficult to attain.

When reversed, this card implies that you're managing too many things at once. You may *think* you're balancing everything well, but others may disagree. On the bright side, this card can be a sign to let some things go so that you can rest and regroup. You may have taken on more than you can handle, but this card is telling you that letting something go will work out just fine.

THREE OF PENTACLES

This card centers on teamwork. The three figures stand in a cathedral where the stonemason on the left is hard at work. To the right are two architects showing the stonemason their plans. Together they'll do an amazing job. Each person has a different skill set and they are of varying ages, but that doesn't stop them from working well together and respecting each other's status and experiences. Underneath the buttress are three carefully carved pentacles indicating harmony among all parties.

Upright, this card signifies the necessary components to complete a plan. The idea reflected in the Ace of Pentacles is now being put into action. When pulled in a reading, this card is telling you to get your resources in order. It's a time to determine what pillars need to be in place for your plan to come to fruition. Perhaps you'll need time and money or patience and persuasion. Whatever it is you need, now is the time to determine and gather

it. In spellwork, use this to gain clarity on what you need to implement your plan.

Reversed, this card denotes tension in a team setting. Perhaps you have a group project to work on but the other participants are putting in either too much or not enough work to be successful. You may be involved in a group, but there's tension between some of the members. As a result, every collective goal fails. When this happens, use this card to foster the necessary harmony required for success.

Having money is imperative to living a healthy and secure life. No matter how you slice it, access to money makes anyone's life easier thanks to the way the global economy is structured. However, money isn't the answer to everything. In fact, the love of money is the root of all evil. The Four of Pentacles reminds us that it can also be the root of regression. Illustrated on the card is a royal who's tightly holding on to their pentacles. One is balanced on their head, another tightly held in their arms, and the final two placed firmly at the bottom of their feet. The figure sits alone and immobile.

When upright, this card signifies the result of hard work and also a tendency toward materialism. In order to attain four pentacles, you must have worked very hard and steadily, making the right choices and ultimately coming out on top. However, the pain of discomfort from that hard work may also leave you fearful of losing all that you worked for or—even worse—becoming too preoccupied with money that you ignore everything else.

When reversed, the Four of Pentacles denotes letting go of that scarcity mindset. Take a step back and see whether you actually need to be so cautious and where the caution is coming from. Have you been destitute in the past? Have you had sudden, unexpected loss? Sift your way through your trauma and recognize that the past doesn't always dictate the future. You will thrive.

M oving across the landscape are two poor individuals. The one on the left uses crutches to walk around on bandaged feet. They lack a coat or any outer clothing for warmth. Based on their face, it looks like they're unwell. The individual to the right is shoeless and wearing a thin, tattered blanket as they both walk through the snow. A church stands to the side of them, fully lit inside. Five pentacles are in the stained-glass window right above the two people, signaling that the church can be a safe haven for them.

Upright, the Five of Pentacles represents sickness and destitution. Luck has run out and there's not much in the way of support. This card may represent that you're going through an extraordinarily difficult time but are handling it all on your own without any help. The lit church window is a sign that help is nearby if you just reach out for it. Use this card to help you take the first step.

Reversed, the Five of Pentacles represents the end to a difficult period. If you're currently in it, it will end soon. You may get a windfall or someone may be generous toward you and offer you some kindness. Or your hard work may be paying off enough to get you to a better situation. This card is a reminder to be grateful for those who have shown you compassion and to pass it on to others whenever you can.

SIX OF PENTACLES

The Six of Pentacles represents someone who is able to give to others while still maintaining their financial position. This card features a wealthy individual with a scale in one hand and the other hand giving money to a person experiencing poverty. Their elaborate and vibrant clothing indicates their status and the many coins they're giving away highlights the extent of their wealth. Similar to modern-day charities, this individual weighs, using a scale to determine how much money they will distribute.

In the upright position, the Six of Pentacles denotes having accumulated enough wealth to freely give to others. This could manifest in a scholarship being paid for, food banks, or other charities that help those less fortunate. Perhaps you're now in a position to help those around you or you may be at the mercy of a charitable organization yourself. Or you may have been essential in securing a grant. In spellwork, this can represent the redistribution of wealth from those who can spare it to those who need it.

In reverse, the Six of Pentacles can signify giving too much away. Perhaps you feel pressured by your family to give more and more of your paycheck to the detriment of your own life and finances. Or you may have been so generous that you miscalculated how much money you can actually spare. This card can be a warning to take care of yourself first before others. Though you may want to give, there's no point in harming yourself for the benefit of someone else.

Illustrated on the Seven of Pentacles is a gardener leaning on their gardening tool, looking quite fatigued. Before them is a vibrant plant decorated with six pentacles. After much tending to, the plant stands tall and looks like it will grow even more. Below the gardener is a single pentacle that represents either another investment or a small token the gardener will take for themselves. The gardener looks tired, indicating that they've worked hard for all they have.

In the upright position, the Seven of Pentacles encourages you to take a step back and focus on long-term investments. It's easy to take life day by day and not look into the future. After all, the future isn't promised. But it's important to plan for the future because it'll arrive sooner than you think. This card can also indicate that you may be investing too much time in a dead end and you should turn your efforts to something that will provide more returns. When making investments, carry this card with you along with a green crystal for luck and money.

Though the Suit of Pentacles deal more with money, this card represents investments in business and also relationships, so if you see it in the reverse, the message may be that you've made a bad investment in either of those categories. It may be hard to hear, but it's actually a blessing. You know to reexamine your life and see where you need to pull back. In spellwork, you can use this card to spur your intuition.

EIGHT OF PENTACLES

O n the Eight of Pentacles is a worker carefully crafting pentacles. They're in deep concentration, giving special care to each pentacle. The worker has chosen to work in isolation as indicated by the nearby town in the background. The pentacles hanging on the tree before the worker show how hard they've been working up until this point. Time and dedication are required in order to master any skill or accomplish any task.

Upright, this card denotes that you may need to work extra hard to meet any goals you have for yourself. Perhaps you want to learn a new skill or you want to take on a new venture; either way, the Eight of Pentacles implies that you'll need to really apply yourself to get what you want. You may want to become even more proficient in your field and this card is telling you to go for it, but be aware that it'll take a lot of hard work. In spellwork, use this card to support you in your efforts.

In reverse, the Eight of Pentacles signifies that you're unrealistically aiming for perfection. Perhaps you've wanted to perfect your craft before starting on a first major project. This can lead to not actually starting the project because you never feel like you're good enough. This card warns you that hard work is good but don't put that above achieving your goals. Perfection isn't the be-all and end-all. In spellwork, use this as a reminder to trust your skills and drive.

NINE OF PENTACLES

Nearing the end of the numerical cards, the Nine of Pentacles represents the penultimate phase before reaching fulfillment. Amid a garden of grapes and pentacles stands a rich person adorned in a long, flowing dress interacting with their pet bird. They seem to be reveling in their wealth, as indicated by them touching one of their pentacles. In the background is a yellow castle matching their garb. This likely means the castle belongs to the affluent person. They're in a position where they're comfortable and reaping the benefits of their investments.

In the upright position, the Nine of Pentacles symbolizes financial freedom that comes as a result of hard work, wise decisions, and luck. When pulled in a reading, this can indicate that you will soon reach this level of freedom. If you've already reached this point, this card indicates that you can treat yourself a little. You deserve it. In spellwork, pair this card with coins and a green candle to help you attain this level of independence.

In reverse, the Nine of Pentacles signifies pursuing the appearance of wealth but actually being in debt. There is pressure to keep up with others on social media. Showing off wealth and expensive purchases is a normal occurrence on certain parts of the internet. If pulled in a reading, this card can indicate that you're putting yourself into debt by trying to look the part. When this comes up, take a step back and look at what's really important: impressing others or actual financial security.

TEN OF PENTACLES

The Ten of Pentacles is the end of a long, arduous, yet rewarding journey. The family elder sits comfortably looking at everything they own. They live in an ornate house decorated with family crests. In front of them stand their children and grandchild as well as their two pet dogs. Decorated around the scene are ten pentacles. The scene signifies an elder who has worked their whole life to provide a comfortable life for themselves and their family. Now they can rest and enjoy the fruits of their labor.

When upright, this card indicates stability, comfort, and happiness. You've put in the labor and now it's time to enjoy yourself. If you haven't reached this point yet, the Ten of Pentacles is telling you to take comfort because this is in your future. It may also indicate that you will become the provider of your family. Perhaps you've wanted to help them in a significant way and this is your time to do so. You're in a position to share your spoils with them, benefiting everyone. In spellwork, this card can be used to manifest your monetary desires.

When reversed, the Ten of Pentacles denotes the feeling of being bound to your wealth. On the card, the elder sits away from their children as if putting them at a distance. *Their* clothes look fancy and intricate but the family's clothes don't. This can indicate a certain level of greed that prevents them from fully investing in their relationships.

PAGE OF PENTACLES

Beneath the Page is a verdant landscape filled with flowers and trees. Everything is at peace and there's nothing but growth to be seen. The Page stands relaxed, wistfully gazing at the pentacle in their hands. They're filled with youthful hope and imagination. From the look on the Page's face, it seems as though they are wistfully envisioning their future and have hope for it. In the distance is a blue mountain signifying the rough journey ahead.

When upright, the Page denotes the beginning of a new venture, similar to the Ace of Pentacles. Unlike that card, however, the Page represents someone who's beginning to understand finances in a tangible way. They may have been unaware in the past, but now they've been inspired to grow their finances. The Page shares qualities with a student: someone willing to learn and work their way toward wisdom. Carry this card with you while fortifying your knowledge to inspire you and aid your research.

When reversed, this card signifies someone who has their head in the clouds but no actual plan to implement their ideas. The thought of having financial stability remains that way—a thought. When pulled in a reading, this can indicate that you're thinking too much about how to begin your financial journey but need to put some action behind it. Pair it with the Knight of Swords to give yourself the bravery needed to dive right in without any doubt or hesitation. This is the sign to take the next step.

KNIGHT OF PENTACLES

U nlike in all other Knight cards, the Knight of Pentacles' horse stands completely still. This inaction represents intense thought and planning. Where the Knight of Wands moves forward without much thought, the Knight of Pentacles sits in deep thought to apply their mind and energy. To the side of them is a landscape that has been tilled and laid open. The Knight and their horse are decorated with some leaves, showing growth and a connection to the earth. In the Knight's outstretched hand lies a single pentacle that will be given to the land to multiply.

Upright, this card signifies the routine and dedication it takes to accomplish any of your dreams. Though the Knight doesn't guarantee actualization of your desires, it shows that hard work goes a long way. The Knight also doesn't let their status prevent them from doing labor that might be considered beneath them. They work the fields like anyone else, knowing this is the work that needs to be done. In spellwork, the Knight represents the dedication and humility needed to get right in the weeds and provide a better future for oneself.

Reversed, this card represents overworking. You may know what you need to do for success, but it's all you've been thinking about and it's taking over your life. There's nothing wrong with taking time out to get things done, but this position is a warning not to let work and the pursuit of physical possessions overtake you. Life is so much more than that.

On her throne among the trees and vegetation sits the Queen of Pentacles. Surrounding her are the various colors of Mother Nature. On her throne are various animals, connecting her to the earth, and slightly diagonal to the throne runs a little rabbit, symbolizing fertility and verve. Underneath her crown is a forest-green cloth, symbolizing growth and fortune. The Queen cradles her pentacle adoringly, as though she's appreciative of all she has and what she's been given through the Universe and her position as Queen.

Similar to the Ten of Pentacles, the Queen represents the matriarch of the family who has excelled in her business ventures and has enough wealth to share with her family. She may represent a director of a charity or someone in politics who decides who gets which resources. The Queen has a deep understanding of money and how to utilize it to its highest benefit. For a manifestation spell, have the Queen in a place you see every day.

Reversed, the Queen can represent a desire to funnel money to oneself instead of passing it on to others. This can manifest in diverting funds that *should* be going to others to oneself, or it can denote a time when you should give yourself the blessings you're constantly giving to others. The Queen in this position can also indicate a woman in charge who has decided to cut others off suddenly or completely. This may be a result of her giving too much or recognizing she's being taken advantage of.

KING OF PENTACLES

The last card in the court, the King of Pentacles sits atop his throne decked in robes covered in grapes. His throne is covered in bulls, signifying strength and boldness. In the King's hands he holds a scepter, to indicate his rule, and a pentacle, to indicate his steady wealth. One of his feet is covered in armor, indicating he still has traces of the Knight in him. The King is comfortable with his wealth and is happy with his life.

Upright, the King denotes that whatever financial plan you've come up with has a high chance of success. Your current business pursuits are going to be prosperous. It can also represent you or a mentor with superb knowledge and business sense who has helped you get to where you are today. This can also indicate that you are reaching the end of a goal you've set out for yourself and now you have the knowledge and experience to pull through at the very end. In spellwork, you can use this as a meditation card to manifest success for yourself when everyone else doubts you and your dreams.

Reversed, the King signifies a person with much wealth but who doesn't know how to invest it or handle it carefully. They may be a person who, as soon as they get a check, spends it all on frivolous purchases, possibly gambling it all away. They don't know how to control themselves and are only concerned with short-term profits rather than long-term benefits.

Traditional Magical Elements

In general, magic practitioners follow the same routine and use similar instruments. The reason for this is to put yourself in the headspace to perform whatever spell you need. It also allows practitioners to share spells among each other with the understanding that one or all of these steps will take place *before* any given spell. It's part of the ritual. To begin any spell, it's important to set up your space with the proper adornments and accoutrements. Magic doesn't require anything other than the practitioner, but having extra tools at the ready helps build up power and intentions for your spellwork. Traditional magical practices may include:

- Altar
- Magic Cloths
- Matches or Lighters
- Candles
- Cauldron or Fireproof Surface
- Salt
- Incense/Cleansing Sprays
- Book of Light
- Consecrated Pens

In this chapter, you will get a fuller understanding of why and how these magical elements are used and whether or not you can incorporate them into your practice. Most, if not all, of these components can be altered or removed depending on your preferences or needs. Once you've read through this section, you will be able to move forward more confidently.

✳ Altar ✳

Your altar is the foundation to your magical practice. It's the sacred space where you'll be able to literally work your magic. An altar can take many forms. Some witches have dedicated rooms or spaces to practice magic, but others may not be as fortunate. For those witches, they may need to have a portable altar where they pack what they need in a trunk or box that moves from place to place, wherever it needs to go. Altars should be any solid, level space away from air drafts, fire, water, or anything unpredictable that might interfere with your practice.

For many, their altar consists of a magic cloth, candles, crystals, salt, tarot cards, cauldrons, and any other relevant components to their practice. Altars are very customizable. They can be as complex or as minimalist as you want. The rule of thumb is that the altar should make you feel at ease. Add as many or as few items as you want in order to perfect it.

When first creating your altar, use incense or a cleansing spray around the area and then take each component in your hands, close your eyes, and imagine light coming from your hand over the item and purifying it. This infuses each object with your energy and intention so it may be used immediately.

✳ Magic Cloths ✳

A magic cloth is the first object that goes over the altar. If you're working with water, salt, ashes, or anything that may cause a mess, the cloth can catch all that for you and make cleaning much easier and faster. Though that is its practical purpose, the magical purpose is both to set the scene and to add to your intentions.

Magic cloths don't have to be made out of any specific material either; the choice is up to you. Their size, whether big or small, long or short, is also up to you and the shape of your altar.

You may want to embroider or paint your magic altar cloths. Perhaps you want to add a sigil, your initials, or any other magical shapes like circles, squares, or mandalas to aid your practice. Of course, you can always purchase one from an independent seller.

✳ Matches or Lighters ✳

Fire is a constant in many witches' magical practices. They're needed to not only light candles—another common staple—but also to light incense or burn herbs, paper, and other flammable objects. Because magic is about the earth and nature, it's preferred to use matches instead of lighters. They're biodegradable and they're easily disposed of. People have been using matches for centuries, so it's another way to be closer to the witches of old.

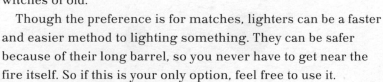

Though the preference is for matches, lighters can be a faster and easier method to lighting something. They can be safer because of their long barrel, so you never have to get near the fire itself. So if this is your only option, feel free to use it.

✳ Candles ✳

A side from being used as a light source, candles are used for much more in witchcraft. Similar to other elements of basic magic, candles are used to set the scene. There's nothing that can quite compare to a candlelit room. It provides a sense of importance and sanctity. But candles can also boost intuition for any spell. They come in different lengths, sizes, colors, and wax types.

The most common examples are chime candles. They're about 4 inches (10 cm) tall and their burn time is about thirty minutes, but there are also long, tapered candles that may burn for an hour or more. Tea light candles tend to be smaller in both burn time and stature and can be used when on the go because most of them come with their own holders, unlike chime candles.

With candle colors, you can create color combinations depending on what you want to accomplish. If perhaps you want a luck in love spell, you may use a green candle and a pink candle to aid you. Then there are wax types. Chime candles are typically made from paraffin wax, which is a by-product of oil, making it the least eco-friendly type of wax. However, there are other natural waxes available: soy wax, coconut wax, palm wax, and beeswax. If you want to avoid fire altogether, feel free to use electric candles.

When using candles, make sure you place them in candleholders. Some are ceramic, cast iron, or metal. A good holder leaves no wiggle room. For safety, it's also important to use a candle snuffer instead of simply blowing out the candles. The snuffer will quickly extinguish the fire safely.

Fire is frequently used in this book. It's imperative that you never leave any lit candles unattended, keep flammable objects away from any open flames, and keep all fire away from drafts to prevent fire from spreading to other areas of your space.

Cauldron or Fireproof Surface

Cauldrons have been used by witches for centuries. They're classic iconography and seem to be a thing of the past when really many witches today own or use a cauldron or fireproof surface in their practice. Unlike the cauldrons in fairy tales, modern-day cauldrons are typically much smaller and aren't mainly used to make witches' brews. In actuality, they're perfect to burn herbs and use as a catcher for flammable objects. Some witches start fires *in* their cauldrons and add objects to it like tissue paper, which burns cleanly, or use coloring to change the flames from yellow to blue or red.

Cauldrons are typically made of cast iron and come with a handle and a lid to quickly put out a fire if needed. They're particularly hardy and able to handle practically any intended use. Follow cast-iron skillet care to maintain your cauldron.

Cauldrons aren't exclusively used for fire. They can also be used for making Moon water. Moon water is water that has been sitting in moonlight overnight. It's charged with the Moon's energy and is potent in spellwork.

If you cannot find or afford a cauldron, an abalone shell is cheaper and a suitable alternative. It can handle hot elements and is beautiful as well. Depending on the size, it can also serve the same purpose of a cauldron.

✳ Salt ✳

S alt has had a crucial role in our history as people. It's been a
vital substance in our lives, with its uses ranging from a food
preserver, a form of payment, and an ingredient to spiritual rituals.
Today it's a staple in modern-day magic because of its multiple
uses. Salt is connected to the earth because it's collected from
rock cliffs and evaporated ocean water. As a result, salt can be
used in any spell involving the connections between either of those
elements and especially any spell involving Cups or Pentacles.

In witchcraft, salt is predominantly used as a form of protection
against negative spirits or as a purifier. The former can manifest
in pouring a circle of salt around your altar or magical space;
this includes sea salt and black salt, another staple. Black salt is
a combination of sea salt and other substances such as incense
ashes or the ashes of any burnt material used in your cauldron or
other fireproof surface.

The latter can be used to cleanse crystals and other magical
objects. To do so, place crystals, amulets, cards, or any other dry
magical object in a jar or bowl, then cover them with sea salt and
leave them on a windowsill overnight or until the Sun sets. Make
sure to have this magical substance on hand to protect yourself
and clean your space of negative energies.

Incense/Cleansing Sprays

Similar to salt, incense and cleansing sprays are meant to cleanse your space of any current or opposing energies. If you don't have a completely neutral space in your home where you can routinely practice magic, cleansing products are a perfect solution to prepare your space. It's not only to cleanse negative energies but also to clear the space from any previous spells you've performed. For example, if your last spell was a repulsion spell and the next one is a love spell, you'll want to dispel those old intentions from the air.

Incense is a tried-and-true purifier. The best method to picking an incense is to see which herbs they're made of. Lavender and eucalyptus, for example, are perfect for purifying; however, you can pick any one you want as long as the scent pleases you. In addition to being a purifier, it's meant to set the mood. You can pick one whose herbs match the intention of your spell.

Alternatively, if you can't use incense because of the smoke, you can make a cleansing spray. A classic and simple recipe is to add 1 teaspoon (5 g) of sea salt to 8 ounces (236 ml) of water, stir well to dissolve the salt, then add to an 8-ounce (236 ml) mist bottle. Make sure the salt is completely dissolved before adding it to the spray bottle. When ready, spray the entire area you'll be working on until satisfied.

✳ Book of Light ✳

A witch's Book of Light is similar to a diary. The difference between this Book and a grimoire is that the former is similar to a magic notebook while the latter is similar to an encyclopedia of spells you've performed and any relevant notes attached to them.

What you might document in your Book of Light are the after-effects of a spell, any supernatural occurrences, or as a companion piece to a spell. You may need to create a sigil or jot down your thoughts and wishes that will be used in a spell. The reverse of this would be your Book of Shadows, which deals with darker emotions. If you're experiencing tough times or trying to overcome a difficult situation, you would document that there. Your Book of Light is meant to be positive and for your benefit. You can include darker emotions, if desired, but it's predominantly used to bring things to light, to aid you in your spellwork.

Throughout this tome, you will use your Book of Light many times. Be sure to always pair it with your consecrated pen to match your energy and intention. If possible, use a Book of Light whose pages are easy to tear out because you might be setting some ablaze. Feel free to customize your Book of Light, whether you create it yourself or buy it from someone else.

Consecrated Pens

To get into consecrated pens, we must first get into what consecration means. To consecrate something means to dedicate it to a sacred purpose. In witchcraft, it's crucial to consecrate everything you'll use in your practice. Once a witch has put their stamp on anything, no other witch should use it. Consecrating something means sticking that thing to you, attuning it to your energies, and making it a vital part of your practice.

The reason you will consecrate a pen is because you will use it to write spells and sigils and document your thoughts and feelings in your grimoire and Book of Light. Whenever you bring a new object to your altar or sacred space, you must first cleanse it. You can use salt, incense smoke, or a cleansing spray. Then once the purifying has finished, take the object (in this case, a pen) in your hands and close your eyes. Take several deep breaths to still yourself. Take one final deep breath and envision blue fire coming from your hands and surrounding the pen. Let it begin from the bottom and envelop the pen in fire until every surface is covered. Once that's happened, let the flames go out. Say aloud:

I will never use this pen for anything else outside its magical purpose. May it be attached to me and never be used by another witch.

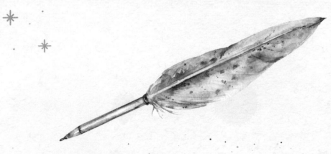

Meditations, Spells, and Rituals

Now that you're familiar with the Major and Minor Arcana and the practices necessary to do magic, you'll now apply that knowledge in the second half of this book. In the following pages you'll find several meditations, spells, and rituals. Each practice has its own benefits and severity when it comes to magic. Depending on the intensity of your spell or how much intention you want to infuse into it, you can perform one, two, or all three types of magic at once. The choice is up to you.

The meditations, spells, and rituals in this chapter cover several topics, such as numbers, love, money, and more. If you want your spells to be particularly complex, you can mix and match any of the spells listed. Tarot magic, much like tarot readings, uses tarot spreads (a specific layout of cards). Each placement in a spread is meant to contextualize the cards' meanings and add an extra layer of intention to every spell for maximum clarity and precision. Use these as a guide if you have better placements in mind.

✳ Meditations ✳

SELF-CONFIDENCE MEDITATION

We are enough all on our own, but there are moments when we forget this. We're constantly told we're not enough in every conceivable way, and eventually, it wears on the spirit. Combine this with the constant comparisons to others and the effects can damage our self-esteem and self-confidence. But falling into this way of thinking doesn't benefit us in the slightest. Confidence and self-assuredness are key to magic and manifestation.

With this meditation, you will call on Strength and pull from the confidence you may not know you have.

Strength

Strength (page 22)
Book of Light
Consecrated pen

1. Ready your altar.

2. Take your Book of Light and consecrated pen and jot down at least five characteristics you like about yourself. Alternatively, or additionally, write down compliments you've received.

3. Lay Strength over the list and gaze at the card.

4. Visualize yourself as the woman on the card and the lion as all the voices that tell you you're lacking. You are the woman trying to silence those voices.

5. Next, say quietly—or aloud—the positive characteristics you wrote down to the lion as a counter to what it says about you.

6. Finish with this affirmation:

> *I am strength, I am strong*
> *This lion and others are wrong*
> *I am worthy, I am enough*
> *I'm not weak; rather, I'm tough.*

WORK THROUGH PAIN

Internal pain is one of the biggest hindrances to life and magic. When turmoil or heartbreak are weighing on the mind, time drags on and it inhibits you from living, from moving on. There are moments when time alone can't heal all wounds. This meditation will help you tackle your inner unease and move toward healing.

GATHER:

Eight of Cups (page 61)
Three of Swords (page 71)
Queen of Cups (page 66)

The High Priestess (page 16)
Consecrated pen
Book of Light

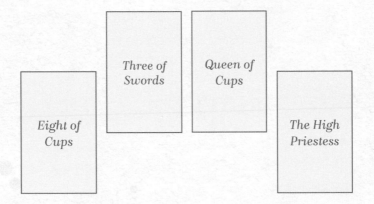

1. Take a few moments to write your anguish down using your consecrated pen in your Book of Light. Be as detailed as you want to be so that it feels cathartic.

2. Place your cards in the order shown on the opposite page.

3. Picture yourself as the figure on the Eight of Cups. The Cups represent your disillusionment. In this meditation, you are moving away from them and on to something better for you.

4. Look at the Three of Swords. This is your current grief. Briefly picture yourself slowly removing the swords from your heart.

5. Turn toward the Queen of Cups and envision yourself as the emotionally mature and regal person on the card. You can and will achieve this.

6. Next, look at the High Priestess and silently ask her to move on your behalf for Spirit. Tap into your intuition.

7. Take a deep breath and picture all of these figures pushing you toward healing and happiness.

ACTUALIZING DREAMS

The main point of magic is to actualize. Everything man-made that has ever existed initially came from the mind as either a wish or a desire to see it come true. Without that initial thought, nothing can be accomplished. This meditation will help you calm your mind, clear it, and then focus on one specific dream you have. Use this meditation as a precursor or a singular practice toward manifestation.

GATHER:

The Magician (page 15)

The Chariot (page 21)

Strength (page 22)

Wheel of Fortune (page 24)

Temperance (page 28)

1 blue candle, for emotions

1 purple candle, for intuition

Matches or a lighter

1. Arrange your altar with the blue candle on the left side and the purple candle on the right. Then place your cards in between them according to the illustration on the page opposite.

2. Next, light both candles, starting with the blue candle.

3. Gaze at The Magician and picture yourself on the card. You have limitless potential and everything you need to begin manifestation. Whatever you don't have will come to you.

4. Turn your attention toward The Chariot. Picture yourself as the rider. No matter what your goals are, you're going to make choices that may advance or hinder your path. Recognize and be at peace with this.

5. Look over at Strength. Picture the lion as whatever hindrances are in your way and yourself as the person who has the calm and grace to tackle any obstacles.

6. Picture the Wheel of Fortune spinning steadily. Most changes aren't drastic, and even the ones you have are surmountable. Know you will oscillate between fortune and misfortune, but stay on target.

7. Lastly, because of the Wheel of Fortune, the path to your dreams may be rocky at times, and that is frustrating. Let Temperance remind you that you must be patient on your journey.

8. After you cycle through these images, say:

> *Spirit, aid my manifestation*
> *I use tarot to achieve elation.*
> *Guide me, show me the way*
> *So I may never waver or stray.*

✴ Quick Number Magic ✴

1 - SPARK INNER CREATIVITY

As we've seen, the number one is predominantly about beginnings and raw potential. This spell can help you activate your subconscious and come up with something new.

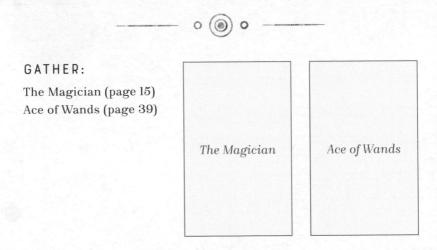

GATHER:

The Magician (page 15)
Ace of Wands (page 39)

1. Arrange your altar with the cards placed according to the illustration above.

2. Hover your hand over The Magician and imagine yourself pulling its essence into your hands.

3. Do the same over the Ace of Wands. Absorb and take in the creativity you have inside yourself and the card. Say:

   I am comprised of talent and passion.
   Nothing can stop me from my creative reaction.

2 - REEVALUATE CURRENT RELATIONSHIPS

Two is a relational number; that applies to magic and humans. Are you putting in more effort in your relationship or not enjoying your time together as much? This spell will reveal the answers.

GATHER:

Two of Cups (page 55)
Two of Swords (page 70)
The High Priestess (page 16)
Written-out name or picture
    of the other person

1. Place the cards according to the illustration. The cards should overlap.

2. Place the written-out name or picture atop the Two of Cups.

3. Look to the Two of Swords. Think of how the relationship makes you feel.

4. Touch The High Priestess card and close your eyes.

5. Intuit what you should do with this relationship. Dig deep.

Two of Cups

Two of Swords

The High Priestess

3 - INSPIRATION FOR COLLABORATION

Teamwork is one meaning of the number three. If your team needs a new perspective on any pressing issues, this spell can bring you the necessary inspiration.

GATHER:

The Empress, Reversed (page 17)

Three of Pentacles (page 86)

Three of Wands (page 41)

Consecrated pen

Paper

1. Using your consecrated pen and the paper, draft your solution and place it on The Empress. Put them on The Empress's spot. Remove your solution.

2. Take the Three of Pentacles and place it horizontally over The Empress. Take your note and say:

> *May my team be hit with*
> *divine inspiration now.*

3. Take the Three of Wands, put it atop the Pentacles, then read your solution aloud. Say:

> *May this bring us closer.*

4 - WHAT DO I
WANT FROM LIFE?

Stability is the most important meaning of four. If you feel unstable most of the time, it may be the moment to look inward and discover what you want from your life.

GATHER:

Four of Swords, Reversed (page 72)

Four of Cups (page 57)

Four of Wands (page 42)

Citrine

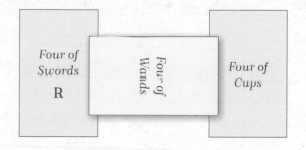

1. Place the Four of Swords in its spot. What swords are you carrying?

2. Next, place the Four of Cups down. Have you become apathetic?

3. Reverse the Cups card to represent introspection.

4. Place the Four of Wands down. This represents time off.

5. Hold the citrine. Envision what makes you happy. Then, say:

   Give me the bravery to chase happiness and stability.

5 - DIVINE ANGER MANAGEMENT

The number five has traditionally negative undertones: conflict, disappointment, and anger. When left unchecked, anger can become destructive. This spell will help you manage your rage.

GATHER:

Five of Wands (page 43)   The Hierophant (page 19)
Five of Cups (page 58)

Five of Wands

Five of Cups

The Hierophant

1. Take the Five of Wands and briefly meditate on the conflict.

2. Take the Five of Cups and exhale any resentment through your mouth.

3. Take the Hierophant and note their need for peace.

4. Put each card in its place and say:

   I banish the anger within me and call upon supernatural peace to move within me.

5. Repeat the incantation aloud as often as needed until you've calmed down.

6 - CAREGIVER INVOCATION

Because six is comprised of both four and two, it covers relationships and stability—two qualities needed when becoming a caregiver. If you'll soon become a caregiver, this spell can aid you in your transition.

GATHER:

Six of Swords (page 74)   Six of Pentacles (page 89)
Six of Cups (page 59)

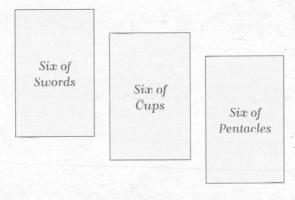

1. Hold the cards and retrieve the Six of Swords. Emotionally prepare for the transition ahead.

2. Regard the Six of Cups. Ponder what your new dependents may need.

3. Take the Six of Pentacles and be aware of your financial responsibility to them.

4. Lay all the cards in their places in the spread and say:

   Fear, be gone as I take on this new responsibility.
   I will move in faith and love.

In tarot, the number seven carries the energies of betrayal and deception. Betrayal leaves a lingering presence that requires a true cleansing to dispel its energies from your space and spirit.

GATHER:

Seven of Swords (page 75)
Seven of Pentacles, Reversed (page 90)
Black salt
Sea salt

Seven of Swords
Seven of Pentacles **R**

1. Take the black salt and encircle your entire space to repel any trace of the traitor.

2. Place the Seven of Swords in its spot. Say:

    (Betrayer's name), you've no place in my life ever again.

3. Put the Seven of Pentacles in its spot. Say:

    I banish you from my home and heart.

4. Pour the sea salt over the cards, and then dispose of all the salt.

8 - CEASE THE PURSUIT OF PERFECTION

Eight's nature of balance and infinity lends itself to the pursuit of perfection. Release yourself from these expectations.

GATHER:

Eight of Pentacles, Reversed
   (page 91)
Eight of Cups (page 61)
Eight of Swords, Reversed
   (page 76)
Strength (page 22)

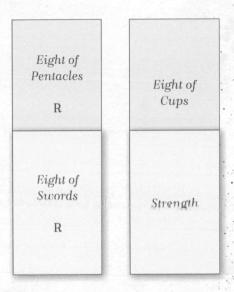

1. Take the Eight of Pentacles. Ask why you must achieve perfection. Put the card in its place.

2. Take the Eight of Cups and say:

    I release the spirit of perfection.

3. Place that card down and then take the Eight of Swords, envisioning yourself removing the binds and blindfold.

4. Put Strength in its place. Say:

    I am perfection. I won't search for what I already possess.

Though worry can feel unmanageable, it can be tamed. This spell can be your starting point to put you in the mindset needed to free yourself of its influence.

GATHER:

Nine of Swords (page 77)
Book of Light
Consecrated pen

Nine of Swords

1. First take your Book of Light and pen. Inscribe all that's currently worrying you. Rip out that paper.

2. Take the Nine of Swords and the ripped paper and place them down in front of you.

3. Read your words aloud, then say:

    Worry will drive me mad no more. I banish these anxieties because they don't serve me in any way. May the flame burn them away and expel them from my heart.

10 - FIND NEW HAPPINESS

Ten is the number of endings and beginnings. In good times, this may sound daunting, but in times of trouble, it's a reminder that life will get better. No matter what, you will find contentment.

GATHER:

Ten of Swords, Reversed
(page 78)
Judgement (page 34)
Ten of Cups (page 63)

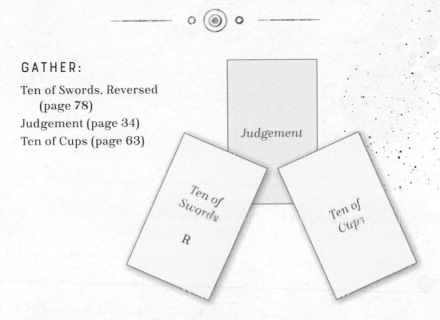

1. The end of this difficult period is near. Place the Ten of Swords in its spot.

2. Place Judgement in its spot. Imagine yourself revived as well.

3. Hold the Ten of Cups and concentrate on it. Thankfully, the end is coming. Say the following and believe it:

   I declare that happiness is in my future.

4. Place this card in its spot.

Love Spells ✳

Love is one of the most intense forms of natural magic there is. But it's also surprisingly elusive, especially in our increasingly lonely societies. We can do our very best and still not find who we're looking for. Though the search can be tiring and even discouraging, if we're meant to have it, it will find its way to us. But we can always use our magic to hurry things along.

In this spell, you'll call upon the Universe and tarot cards to put your wishes out into the world and attract the love you desire.

The Lovers

Wheel of Fortune

Nine of Wands

GATHER:

The Lovers (page 20)
Wheel of Fortune (page 24)
Nine of Wands (page 47)
A tarot card that reflects the
    person you wish to attract

2 pink candles, for love
Matches or a lighter
3 rose quartz crystals, for love

1. Place one candle on each end of your altar and light them, leaving lots of room in between.

2. Place the cards in the order shown opposite.

3. Go through your deck and find a card that represents the person you hope to attract. Once you find it, hold the card to your heart, then place it down.

4. Take each crystal and place them on the first three cards.

5. Close your eyes and envision the first card. Keep in mind this may not be a *literal representation* of the love you want, but recognize it as the spirit of the love you desire. Picture all the love funneling from the Lovers into the rose quartz.

6. Repeat for the Wheel of Fortune and Nine of Wands. Remember, the Wheel of Fortune may take several rotations for you to find your love. The Nine of Wands represents how the journey for companionship, so far, has been arduous. But just like the figure in the card, you can overcome your fatigue and hold on to hope.

7. Once you've done this, place all the crystals on the fourth card (the one you selected) and repeat this incantation:

> *Spirit divine, send me someone I can call mine.*
> *A partner sublime, so we can be together for all time.*

8. Extinguish the candles.

BRAND-NEW RELATIONSHIP BLESSING

New relationships can be simultaneously exciting and nerve-racking. The novelty of a partnership can have you feeling like you can conquer the world but also afraid it might end sooner than you'd like. Using this spell, you will ask Spirit for a blessing and also supply your own.

GATHER:

Two of Cups (page 55)
Three of Swords, Reversed
    (page 71)
Knight of Wands (page 50)

Red magic cloth, for passion
2 white candles, for Spirit
Matches or a lighter

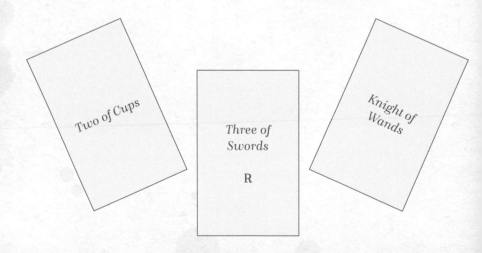

1. Reverently place the red cloth on your altar and think of your pure, novel love.

2. Place your cards in the order shown opposite.

3. Gaze at the Two of Cups and picture you and your new partner as the people on the card, holding hands and looking into each other's eyes. You're no longer alone.

4. Next, peer at the Three of Swords. As you look upon it, know whatever past heartbreak you've experienced won't break this coupling if you're aware of its current effects on you.

5. Lastly, envision yourself as the Knight of Wands, who won't allow fear to prevent you from enjoying this new flame.

6. Place both white candles at the top of the altar. As you light them, say:

O Spirit, send us your blessing and favor
This new love I will savor.
Bring us happiness, bring us love
I call upon you and my magic from above.

7. Extinguish the candles.

UNIFYING FAMILY

Any family, regardless of culture or size, has its moments. There are times when all is well and others when there's a rift separating members. Difficult periods like these may need a supernatural force to mend torn relationships and bitter hearts. Use this spell to soften stone hearts and bring the family back together.

GATHER:

Four of Cups (page 57)
Two of Swords, Reversed
 (page 70)
Five of Cups, Reversed
 (page 58)
Ten of Cups (page 63)

Matches or a lighter
Rose or lavender incense,
 for cleansing
Pink altar cloth, for love
Cleansing spray (optional)

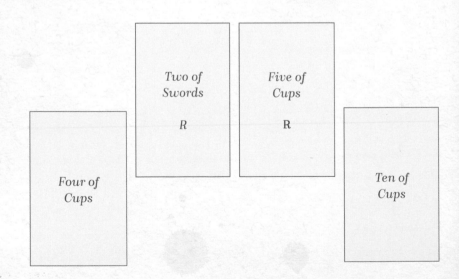

1. When no one's home, light the incense and waft it about the house and then your altar. (You may use a cleansing spray if needed.) Depending on the scent, it may also calm the space of negative energies.

2. Lay the pink cloth across your altar.

3. Place your cards in the order shown opposite.

4. Take the Four of Cups and picture the feuding family members taking the cup offered to them.

5. Grab the Two of Swords and picture the figure swiftly slicing through the conflict.

6. Take the Five of Cups and envision the cups slowly turning up, filling with water, and nourishing the family.

7. Lastly, imagine the water filling the cups in the Ten of Cups, bringing joy and harmony to everyone

8. Hover your hands over the cards, then say:

> *Let their hearts soften and may they drink*
> *from the cups of the Divine.*

9. Extinguish the incense.

SEARCHING FOR FRIENDSHIP

Humans are relational beings. Friendship is a major part of life. Finding friendship in adulthood can be a huge struggle. Similar to romantic love, it can be an issue of luck, timing, and compatibility. For some, making friends is effortless, but for others, it may require an extra boost.

Using this spell, in combination with external efforts, can give you the confidence to put yourself out there and clarify the friends you desire to meet.

GATHER:

Ace of Cups (page 54)
Ace of Swords (page 69)
Three of Cups (page 56)
Book of Light
Consecrated pen
Matches or a lighter
Tongs
Cauldron/fireproof surface

Ace of Cups

Ace of Swords

Three of Cups

1. Take your Book of Light and ask yourself what you look for in a friend; write it down with your consecrated pen. Be as honest as possible. Don't worry about being reasonable; just focus on what you want.

2. Tear that page out and place it in the center of your altar.

3. Take the Ace of Cups in your hand and envision the overflowing water as the joy and contentment you'll feel once you've found your people. Then place it in its spot.

4. Take the Ace of Swords and envision the sword cutting through your hesitation, insecurities, and worries. Then feel the victory you know is coming to you.

5. Take the Three of Cups and picture yourself among the friend group. You can and will have an amazing time with any one of them. When ready, recite:

> *Friendship, friendship, I will attain*
> *New relationships I will gain*
> *Some will fit and some will not*
> *But I'll find people with similar thought.*

6. Light a match, then use the tongs to pick up the list.

7. Take the list and set it aflame over the cauldron/fireproof surface. When you are done, dispose of the ashes in the trash.

Money and Fortune Spells

DISPEL AND BANISH GREED

Whenever money is involved, there's bound to be greed. The love of money truly corrupts even the best of us. Those with a lot of money tend to hoard it and become stingy with it. Instead of properly allocating resources, some underhandedly collect it for themselves, to the detriment of others. When left unchecked, greed has the power to ruin lives. If you notice someone has become overrun with avarice, use this spell to stop them.

Four of Pentacles

Ace of Cups

GATHER:

Four of Pentacles (page 87)
King of Pentacles (page 97)
Ace of Cups (page 54)
Black magic cloth, for repelling
   negative energy
1 brown candle, for grounding
1 black candle, for banishment
Matches or a lighter
Consecrated pen
Book of Light
Sea salt, for purification

King of Pentacles

1. Set the black cloth atop your altar. Arrange the candles so the brown candle is on your left and the black is on your right. Light them.

2. With your consecrated pen, write down the name of the person possessed by greed in your Book of Light, rip that page out, and place it to the side.

3. Place the Four of Pentacles in its spot. Take the name of the person you wrote down, place it on top of the card, and say:

    [Person's name], your greed is corrupting you and it's affecting all around you. It's evil and must be dispelled.

4. Take the King of Pentacles and place that card in its spot. Keep your finger on the card, then say:

    Today, I use this spell to bind you and demand your greed be exhumed.

5. Take the sea salt and pour a circle around the Four of Pentacles and the person's name. Say:

    With this salt I bind your greed and purify you of its effects.

6. Place some of the salt on the person's name and then hover your hand over the Four of Pentacles.

7. Pick up the Ace of Cups and imagine Spirit pouring its power into you. Visualize the cleansing force of water overcoming you.

8. Place the Ace on the Four, then turn them both upside down, symbolizing the person's inevitable transformation.

9. Extinguish the candles.

10. Collect the salt and either wash it down the sink or dispose of it in the trash.

NEW BUSINESS WISH

Venturing out on your own in business can be terrifying. There's more risk, work, and time involved, but for some, it's all worth it to gain freedom and fulfillment. At the beginning of any journey, we can all use a little luck to get us started. This prayer will petition Spirit to bless you with all you need to begin this new venture.

GATHER:

Ace of Pentacles (page 84)

Knight of Pentacles (page 95)

Eight of Pentacles (page 91)

Nine of Pentacles (page 92)

Matches or a lighter

Mint incense

Green aventurine, for attracting luck and success

Eight of Pentacles

Knight of Pentacles

Ace of Pentacles

Nine of Pentacles

1. Light the incense and let the smoke waft through your space. Don't forget to extinguish the fire.

2. Arrange your altar as desired with the necessary components.

3. Place the cards in their designated spots according to the illustration opposite.

4. Take the aventurine and place it on the Ace of Pentacles, directly on the pentacle. Hold your hand over it and imagine that Spirit is infusing the aventurine with divinity.

5. Next, place the crystal on the Knight of Pentacles. Hold your hand over the aventurine and imagine yourself as the Knight, more than willing to put in the hard work needed to make your business successful.

6. Do the same with the Eight of Pentacles and the Nine of Pentacles. Take a deep breath and envision yourself as those people. You are the wealthy, hardworking figure on the card. You will find success.

7. Take the cards and the crystal to your office and set a mini altar there.

LOCATE A NEW ABODE

Housing is a vital part of life, and finding the right home can be difficult depending on income level and availability. When making such a huge decision, it's crucial to have a bit of luck on your side. Take the cards of this spell with you as you make your search and visit any properties.

GATHER:

The Moon (page 32)
Wheel of Fortune (page 24)
The Empress (page 17)
1 green candle, for luck

Matches or a lighter
Consecrated pen
Book of Light

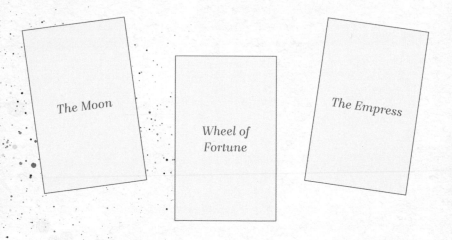

The Moon

Wheel of
Fortune

The Empress

1. Arrange your altar as desired with the listed components.

2. Take the green candle and light it. This should be lit throughout the duration of the spell.

3. Take your consecrated pen and write down the addresses of the places you want to live in your Book of Light. Tear the page out.

4. Place the addresses in the center of the altar.

5. Next, place The Moon on its space according to the illustration opposite. If you're having difficulty picking which home you'd like, gaze upon the card and activate your intuition. Say:

   I call on my inner wolves to aid me in my decision.
   Mother Moon, show me the way I must go and guide me
   toward the best home for me.

6. Now, place the Wheel of Fortune on its spot. Circle your finger over the Wheel as if you're activating it. Say:

   O, Wheel, find me in your favor, and grant me
   the luck I need to complete this task. I wait for your
   opening and will act accordingly.

7. Lastly, move on to The Empress. Say:

   I aim to be like the Empress: happy, secure, and safe.
   I see this for myself and will embody her essence.

8. Look down at the addresses and briefly imagine yourself living in each of those places. Then look back at the flame of the green candle. Say:

   O, Spirit, move through me and grant me the
   knowledge to make the right choice for me.

9. Extinguish the candle.

10. Keep the cards and addresses somewhere you can see them daily until you have made your decision.

MEETING YOUR TWIN FLAME

A twin flame isn't the same thing as a soulmate. The latter has romantic undertones, but a twin flame is simply someone who will change the trajectory of your life. This person *could* be an intimate partner, but could also be a mentor, mentee, friend, or familiar. You know you've met them when it feels incredible and like kismet.

GATHER:

Two of Cups (page 55)
Three of Cups (page 56)
Knight of Wands (page 50)
Ten of Cups (page 63)

Matches or a lighter
2 pink candles, to represent relationships

1. Arrange your altar as desired.

2. Pick up the Two of Cups. Say:

   I use this card to call out to my twin flame. May our relationship be equal and mutually beneficial.

3. Place the Two in its designated spot according to the illustration opposite.

4. Next, pick up the Three of Cups. Say:

   If our relationship is platonic, may we have fun and understand each other deeply.

5. Place the card in its designated spot.

6. Pick up the Knight of Wands. Say:

   I ask for the spirit of the Knight to charge into the relationship and not hide from its intensity.

7. Place the card in its designated spot.

8. Pick up the Ten of Cups. Say:

   O, Spirit, bless me with the union. I will cherish the time spent with my twin flame and I hope they will also.

9. Light one candle and then use it to light the other, signifying the energy one person gives to another.

10. Allow the candles to fully burn down in their holders to complete the spell.

11. Wait a while before touching the holders and then dispose of the wick in the trash.

✳ Third-Eye Spells ✳

OPEN YOUR THIRD EYE

When talking about the "third eye," we're referring to the third-eye chakra, which rests in the middle of your forehead just above the space in between your eyebrows. It's the chakra that deals with intuition, psychic powers, dreams, and even visions. Some people can tap into their intuition effortlessly and others need a little bit of help. This spell will help you utilize your third eye, beginner or not.

GATHER:

The High Priestess (page 16)
The Hanged Man (page 26)
Seven of Cups (page 60)
Matches or a lighter

Frankincense incense, to provoke intuition
Salt spray (optional)
1 purple candle, to represent the third eye

1. Light the incense and quickly extinguish the flame. Imagine its smoke raising the vibrational energy of the space, setting the scene. (A salt spray will also suffice.)

2. Clear your altar with the intention to place the cards as shown in the illustration opposite.

3. Take The High Priestess and move your gaze across the symbolism: the pomegranates, pillars, and Moon at her feet. Imagine her awakening your intuition.

4. Next, take The Hanged Man and picture yourself as the man, choosing to open your mind to find an alternative perspective.

5. Lastly, gaze at the Seven of Cups to invoke prophetic dreams, then arrange the cards in their designated spots.

6. Place the purple candle in the center of the cards and light it.

7. Stare into the flame and imagine the same light behind your third eye. Feel its heat, then say:

I call on thee, open!

8. When you're done, extinguish the candle.

CONTACTING ANCESTORS

We're the culmination of our ancestors; every person, decision, mistake, and journey has resulted in our existence. When searching for a spirit guide or mentor, your ancestors are a great place to start. Because they're connected to you and your history, they have valuable insight for you. This spell will allow you to reach out to them and make contact.

GATHER:

Death (page 27)
Judgement (page 34)
The Hermit (page 23)
1 purple candle, for reaching
    into the spirit world
Matches or a lighter
1 white candle, to contact the spirits
A picture or object of (or a tarot card
    similar to) the person you wish
    to contact

The Hermit

Judgement

Death

1. Place the purple candle to the left of you, then light it. Say:

   With this candle, I light the veil separating worlds.

2. Next, place the white candle to your right and light it. Say:

   *With this candle, I light my way into the spirit
   world toward my ancestors.*

3. Arrange the cards in accordance with the illustration opposite.

4. Touch each card in order, starting with Death. It represents the transition your ancestors have already finalized. Next, touch Judgement. Your ancestors may have lived unfulfilling lives and this represents their desire to find their purpose. Lastly, touch The Hermit. This card represents the wisdom your ancestors contain within them.

5. Take the object/picture/tarot card representing the ancestor you wish to contact. Hold it and focus your gaze on it. Place it in its spot.

6. Say their name aloud and ask them to come to you and show you a sign they're there with you.

7. Be patient until they've made contact. From there, ask them whether they'd like to be your spirit guide. If they say yes, thank them. If no, repeat this spell from step 5 with another person in mind.

8. When you're ready, extinguish the candles.

NEW BEGINNINGS
SAMHAIN SPELL

This sabbat, commonly known as Halloween in the Northern Hemisphere and on April 30/May 1 in the Southern Hemisphere, is the pagan New Year. This holiday's perfect for abandoning the past and inviting new spirits to guide you. Samhain is also the most powerful time to use magic, even more so during the Full Moon.

GATHER:

Death (page 27)
Ace of Wands (page 39)
Eight of Cups (page 61)
The Empress (page 17)
The Emperor (page 18)
1 black candle, for endings
1 white candle, for beginnings

1 green candle, for new journeys
1 silver candle, for feminine
    spirit guides
1 gold candle, for masculine
    spirit guides
Matches or a lighter

Death	Ace of Wands	Eight of Cups	The Empress	The Emperor

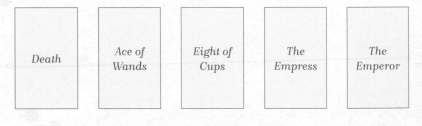

Remember, always use candleholders. If using electric candles, place a crystal or colored paper in front of each candle to differentiate the colors that correspond with the candles noted above.

1. Find a flat, sturdy surface to perform the spell.

2. Place the cards in their spots according to the illustration opposite.

3. Place each candle on or above its corresponding card in this order: black for Death, white for the Ace of Wands, green for the Eight of Cups, silver for The Empress, and gold for The Emperor.

4. As you light the black candle, say:

> *I light the spirit of Death. May all that no longer serves me be left behind in the old year.*

5. Take the black candle, use it to light the white candle, and say:

> *I light the beginning of the new year.*
> *I spark the genesis of this chapter.*

6. Take the white candle and use it to light the green candle. Then say:

> *I begin my journey into this next phase, full of purpose and intention.*

7. Use the green candle to light the silver candle and say:

> *O, Empress, be my spirit guide. I ask you to give me fruitfulness and guide me toward the actions I must take.*

8. Use the silver candle to light the gold candle and say:

> *O, Emperor, provide me with stability, power, and protection. Show me when to stick to my convictions and respond with reason.*

9. Envision each card pouring themselves into you to transform you.

10. Extinguish the candles.

CLEANSING
CANDLEMAS RITUAL

Candlemas, celebrated on February 1 in the Northern Hemisphere and on August 1 in the Southern Hemisphere, marks the final day of winter and the beginning of spring. The earth is beginning to awaken and spring is on the horizon. Naturally, winter is a time of rest and dormancy, but spring is a time of rebirth and action. Shake yourself free of winter's fatigue and take the time to cleanse yourself and your space of old energies so you may welcome in the breath of spring.

GATHER:

Death (page 27)

The Empress (page 17)

Straw broom, for cleaning

Rosemary incense, for cleansing

Matches or a lighter

1 pine-scented candle, to represent winter

1 floral-scented candle, to represent spring

Seeds of any kind, to represent the beginning of spring

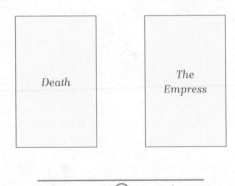

Death

The Empress

Alternatives to this spell are a regular plastic-bristled broom, salt spray, and electric candles.

1. In classic witch fashion, use the straw broom to sweep your entire space of dirt and dust. If possible, dump the debris outside. If not, a trash can will do.

2. Open the windows of your home to let the old energies out and new energies in.

3. Once done, close the windows, light the incense, then walk through each room, one by one, allowing the smoke to permeate every corner.

4. Take the remaining listed supplies and bring them to the biggest room in your home. Arrange the cards according to the illustration opposite. Place the pine-scented candle above Death (which represents the end of winter) and the floral-scented candle above The Empress (which represents Brigid, the goddess of Candlemas). Spread the seeds along the altar however you desire.

5. Light the pine-scented candle and place your finger on Death. Look at the card, then say:

    O, Death, continue your march and bring winter to its end.

6. Repeat for the next candle and card. Say:

    O, Brigid, goddess and empress of spring. Carry me into your embrace and bring renewal to the earth.

7. Leave the candles lit and pray to Brigid. Tell her your wishes for the upcoming season.

8. When you are finished, dispose of the seeds in the trash.

9. Extinguish the candles.

BELTANE
SUMMER CELEBRATION

Summer is on the horizon! This sabbat, celebrated on May 1 in the Northern Hemisphere and on October 31 in the Southern Hemisphere, is a huge time of celebration. Beltane introduces summer, the most active and delightful time of the year, so it's a particularly joyous time for witches. Most celebrate this sabbat with a bonfire large enough to dance around. The day ends with a night-long party. However, if you want to celebrate on a smaller scale, this ritual will scratch that itch. Ideally, perform this spell during sunset.

GATHER:

The World (page 35)
The Sun (page 33)
Four of Wands (page 42)
Three of Cups (page 56)
Red, orange, or yellow clothes, to represent fire and celebratory colors
Fun, happy music
1 red candle
1 orange candle
1 yellow candle
Matches or a lighter

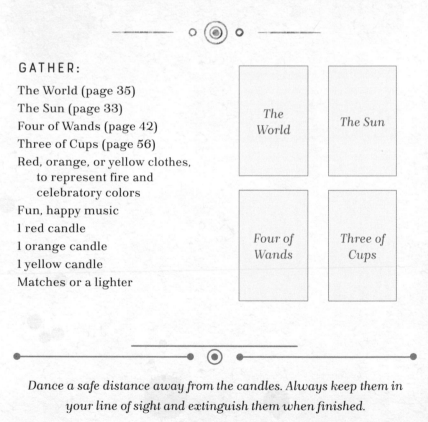

Dance a safe distance away from the candles. Always keep them in your line of sight and extinguish them when finished.

1. Don your festive clothes. Make sure they're comfortable and provide ease of movement.

2. Turn on the music and turn your attention to The World. It's the clear symbol that spring is ending and summer is coming, bringing warmth and joy. Lift the card to the sky and then place it in its designated spot according to the illustration opposite. •

3. Turn your attention to The Sun, a clear representation of summer. If possible, look toward the actual Sun and know it will soon dominate the sky, bringing a bounty of experiences and harvest. Place the card in its designated spot.

4. Next, turn your attention to the Four of Wands, which represents celebration. Take all the passion and anticipation you have for the summer and turn it into a jubilant dance. Place the card in its designated spot.

5. Lastly, turn your attention to the Three of Cups, which represents contentment with friends. Picture your friends or loved ones as the figures on the card. Envision all the fun and excitement you'll experience this season. Place the card in its designated spot.

6. Arrange your candles in any order you please. Light them with matches and let the music sway you. Feel your joy and excitement, your hopes and wishes for this holiday, and let them carry you.

7. When ready, extinguish the candles.

LAMMAS OFFERING RITUAL TO HABONDIA

Habondia is the queen of all witches. She's also the goddess of abundance and generosity. Habondia rules over Lammas, celebrated on August 1 in the Northern Hemisphere and on February 1 in the Southern Hemisphere. This sabbat is the beginning of the first harvest. The summer solstice has passed and the Sun is slowly losing its power. From now on the days will be longer and eventually grow colder. Enjoy this warm season while it's still here. With this ritual, thank the goddess for all she's given.

GATHER:

Ace of Pentacles (page 84)
Ten of Pentacles (page 93)
Death (page 27)
The Hermit (page 23)

Photo of Habondia
Summer fruits, vegetables, and/or bread, to act as offerings
Cauldron

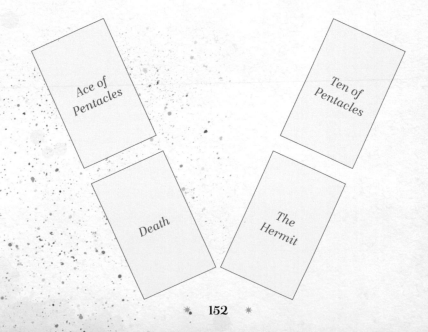

1. Place a photo of Habondia at the top center of the altar.

2. Take the Ace of Pentacles, which represents the beginning of harvest, and imagine the hand of the Divine giving you the pentacle, the symbol of health and wealth. You'll retain this for the rest of the season.

3. Take the Ten of Pentacles, which represents abundance and family, and see yourself as any one of the people on the card, enjoying what Habondia has provided you and your loved ones.

4. Take the Death card, which represents the end of summer. Gaze upon it and anticipate the end of this season. Savor the moment.

5. Lastly, take The Hermit, which represents future introspection. The Hermit is the harbinger of winter and the "dark period" of the earth.

6. Place the cards in their designated spots according to the illustration opposite.

7. Now, take all the summer bounty and place it into your cauldron.

8. Put the cauldron in between the cards and say:

   O, Habondia, goddess of abundance, I present to you this
   offering for your gifts and generosity. Thank you for your gifts.
   I celebrate you today with this reciprocity.

9. Leave the offering until the end of Lammas. When the time comes, compost the offering.

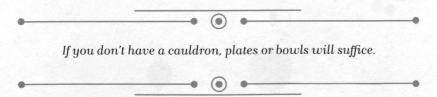

If you don't have a cauldron, plates or bowls will suffice.

EPILOGUE

Within these pages, I hope you have found
Yourself confident, magical, spellbound.

The cards tell a story, you tell your own,
Using this volume as your stepping-stone,

To deepening your practice and craft
To lengthen, to create, or to redraft,

The details of your future, your life
Despite the ups, the downs, the strife.

Now take your wisdom and what you have learned
Ahead with you, leave no card left unturned.

So mote it be.

Acknowledgments

L ike the many faces of the tarot, various magical people are
responsible for the manifestation of this book. Each brings
their own knowledge, story, and influence to create this
bewitched tome.

I'm so grateful to Sara Bonacum, who believed in me; without
her, this book would not exist. She has blessed me with her
kindness and encouraging words. I hope this book honors you.

To my editor, Elizabeth You, thank you for taking this book and
adding your own enchantment to my words. To Cara Donaldson
and those on the Quarto team, thank you for your creativity,
efforts, and passion for your work.

I also thank all the witches who have shared their spells,
knowledge, and experiences online to improve the community
as a whole and who have been cited in this book. I admire your
openness and desire to help others. You've certainly helped me.

Lastly, to my two darling familiars, Sabrina and Santana, and
my adoring husband, Nathan, who offered a listening ear and a
warm smile. Your love keeps me going every single day.

Resources and References

Biddy Tarot. Accessed April 26, 2023. https://www.biddytarot.com.

Carlson, Jess. "Manifest with Simple Tarot Spells." *Jess Carlson: Make Your Own Magick* (Blog), April 5, 2014. https://jesscarlson.com/simple-tarot-spells.

Caro, Tina. "A Guide to Cleansing Herbs Magic." *Magickal* (Blog), last updated November 24, 2022. https://magickalspot.com/cleansing-herbs-magic.

Ceridwen. "Wiccan Holidays: Wheel of the Year Explained (with 2023 Dates)." *Craft of Wicca: Ancient Practices for a Modern World* (Blog), accessed April 26, 2023. https://craftofwicca.com/wiccan-holidays-wheel-of-the-year-explained.

Della, Jamie. *The Book of Spells: The Magick of Witchcraft.* Emeryville, CA: Ten Speed Press, 2019.

G., Bev. "Tarot Cards as a Tool for Magic: Tips and Tricks for Effective Spellcasting." *Exemplore*, March 26, 2023. https://exemplore.com/fortune-divination/Create-Your-Own-Tarot-Spells-and-Rituals.

"Habondia (Or Habundia)." Encyclopedia.com, accessed April 26, 2023. https://www.encyclopedia.com/science/encyclopedias-almanacs-transcripts-and-maps/habondia-or-habundia.

Hayn, Lyza. "19 Herbs for Good Luck & Prosperity (+ How to Use Them In Your Life)." *outofstress* (Blog), last updated November 27, 2022. https://www.outofstress.com/herbs-for-good-luck.

Herb, Melissa. "How to Cast Spells with Tarot Cards." *Astro Pagan* (Blog), hosted on Medium, September 8, 2021. https://astropagan.com/how-to-cast-spells-with-tarot-cards-94eb64b26970.

The Individualogist Team. "Tarot Spells and Tarot Magic: A Complete Guide."
Individualogist (Blog), January 12, 2019. https://individualogist.com/
tarot-spells-and-magic-guide.

Jenwytch. "Southern Hemisphere Sabbat Dates." *Spheres of Light* (Blog),
accessed April 26, 2023. https://spheresoflight.com.au/SOL/
sabbat-dates.

Labryinthos (Blog). Accessed April 26, 2023. https://labyrinthos.co.

Patterson, Rachel. "Tarot Spells." *John Hunt Publishing* (Blog),
November 5, 2018. https://www.johnhuntpublishing.com/blogs/
moon-books/tarot-spells.

Pollux, Amaria. "10 Powerful Money Herbs and How to Use Them."
Wicca Now (Blog), accessed April 26, 2023. https://wiccanow.com/
top-10-most-powerfull-money-herbs-and-how-to-use-them.

Rosetta. "Tarot Card Magic: 3 Easy Spells to Try. *Charm Your Life | Tarot +
Magic* (Blog), accessed April 26, 2023. https://www.tarotrosetta.com/
the tarot-blog/tarot-card-magic-spells.

Tarot (Blog). Accessed April 26, 2023. https://www.tarot.com.

"Tarot Spells." *Free Witchcraft Spells* (Blog), June 20, 2022.
https://freewitchspells.com/tarot-spells.

Thomas, Sophie Saint. "What Is a Twin Flame, and How Is It Different from a
Soul Mate?" *Allure*. April 28, 2022. https://www.allure.com/story/
what-is-a-twin-flame.

Wigington, Patti. "Salt Folklore and Magic: Using Salt in Modern Pagan
Traditions." *Learn Religions* (Blog), April 2, 2018.
https://www.learnreligions.com/salt-folklore-and-magic-2562502.

Wigington, Patti. "Tarot Card Spells." *Learn Religions* (Blog), April 9, 2018.
https://www.learnreligions.com/tarot-card-spells-2562774.

Index